Teach a Child to Read with Children's Books

Combining story reading, phonics, and writing to promote reading success

Second Edition

by Mark B. Thogmartin

Family
Literacy
Center

ERIC Clearinghouse on Reading,
English, and Communication

EDINFO Press

Published in 1997 by
ERIC Clearinghouse on Reading, English, and Communication
Carl B. Smith, Director
2805 East 10th Street, Suite 150
Bloomington, IN 47408-2698
and
EDINFO Press
P.O. Box 5247
Bloomington, IN 47407

Editor: Eleanor C. Macfarlane
Design and Production: David J. Smith and Kathleen McConahay
Cover Design: David J. Smith
Cover Photo: CLEO Photography
All inside photos by CLEO Photography except pages 23, 55, and 111 by
Mark B. Thogmartin; pages vii and 67 by Jeffrey Thogmartin; and page 91
by Robert Congdon.

ERIC (an acronym for Educational Resources Information Center) is a national network of 16 clearinghouses, each of which is responsible for building the ERIC database by identifying and abstracting various educational resources, including research reports, curriculum guides, conference papers, journal articles, and government reports. The Clearinghouse on Reading, English, and Communication (ERIC/REC) collects educational information specifically related to reading, English, journalism, speech, and theater at all levels. ERIC/REC also covers interdisciplinary areas, such as media studies, reading and writing technology, mass communication, language arts, critical thinking, literature, and many aspects of literacy.

This publication was prepared with partial funding from the Office of Educational Research and Improvement, U.S. Department of Education, under contract no. RR93002011. Contractors undertaking such projects under government sponsorship are encouraged to express freely their judgment in professional and technical matters. Points of view or opinions, however, do not necessarily represent the official view or opinions of the Office of Educational Research and Improvement.

Library of Congress Cataloging-in-Publication Data

Thogmartin, Mark B. (Mark Bruce), 1956–
   Teach a child to read with children's books : combining story reading,
phonics, and writing to promote reading success / by Mark B. Thogmartin.
—2nd ed.
      p.   cm.
   Includes bibliographical references and index.
   ISBN 1-883790-25-5 (pbk.)
   1. Reading (Early childhood) 2. Early childhood education—Parent participation. 3. Reading—Phonetic method. 4. Individualized instruction. 5. Home
schooling. I. Title.
LB1139.5.R43T46 1997
372.4—dc21
                                                        97-21001
                                                        CIP

Teach a Child to Read with Children's Books

Table of Contents

Foreword

by Jim Trelease

For anyone teaching reading, Mark Thogmartin's book *Teach a Child to Read with Children's Books* should be required reading. A veteran teacher, Thogmartin presents a common-sense argument that is widely supported by extensive research: Real books offer greater success than textbooks.

To begin with, real books like *The House That Jack Built* or *Miss Nelson Is Missing* have the same 44 sounds and syllables, phonics and sight words as do textbooks. The big difference is that real books are a whole lot more interesting. Have you ever heard of a child with a favorite basal reader or a favorite vowel or consonant? Of course not; they have favorite stories and favorite authors.

In all teaching, the greatest amount of learning takes place at the point of interest. Without interest, the whole process becomes a case of forced-feeding. And as Plato noted, "Forced feeding always turns the stomach."

For home-schoolers, *Teach a Child to Read with Children's Books* should be a second bible in the family, filled with resources, information, strategies, and inspiration for learning. I highly recommend it.

Foreword

by Carl B. Smith, Director
Family Literacy Center and
ERIC Clearinghouse on Reading, English, and Communication

Whether you are a home-schooler or a parent who works regularly with your children on their reading and writing homework, you naturally look for new ideas that will help you and your children be more effective. That's what this book does—gives you new ideas and techniques that you may not have in your background.

If you are like most parents, you rely on your own learning in order to help your children. If those techniques worked for you, why not use them with your children? Isn't that your logic? There's nothing wrong with those thoughts, but you must admit that they limit you to your own experience.

What if your child doesn't learn exactly in the same way that you did? What if your children do not have the same cultural experiences that you had, or what if they have a personality that responds to reading and to writing differently from yours? These are the reasons, of course, that we parents continue to explore different ways to motivate and to educate our children.

Phonics, for example, is well known as a successful technique for helping young readers unravel the relationship between the sound of words and their spellings. Formal research studies confirm the value of phonics knowledge as a means for identifying printed words, but there is no single approach that guarantees success, and there are other highly important aspects involved in learning to read. How to process written information and how to enjoy reading are two examples.

In this book, Mark Thogmartin, educator and parent, offers techniques and strategies that parents can use to give their children a balanced approach to reading and writing. He shows parents how to use the best of children's literature to stimulate interest in story reading while at the same time developing basic decoding and grammatical skills. By using his experience with his own children and his personal re-search into tutoring techniques, he opens the windows to fresh thinking about both the methodology and the content of reading and writing instruction.

You will find that Mark Thogmartin explains his think-ing behind his approach in the initial chapters of this book. Then he presents a series of specific ideas to show how to carry out this balance between using books and teaching skills. We applaud his message that promotes the joy of reading at the same time that children learn basic skills.

Dedication

With love and gratitude to my wife, Donna, and to my three sons, Ryan, Jeffrey, and Philip for patiently giving up so much of their time for and with me.

Acknowledgments

I've had a nasty habit in the past of not reading the author's acknowledgments in the fronts of the books I've read. No more! I certainly am not acquainted with the folks thanked by the authors of these books but, from now on, I will reflect back to all the help I received from the people below as I read those anonymous lists of faceless names. I now know just how important support, critical advice, and professional assistance can be in a project such as this. Here's my list and, let me assure you, these people have faces covered with sweat because of the help they gener-ously gave to me.

My wife, Donna, put in many hours at home and in the library researching and typing the bibliography of children's books. My father and mother, who live next door, supported us in a thousand different ways. Marcy Ledford, my original Reading Recovery® teacher leader, first convinced me of the value of this kind of reading instruction. Paula Connor and Mary Fried, two other Reading Recovery® leaders, have helped to sharpen my skills, and they gave very specific advice on the manuscript. Dr. Evelyn Freeman at Ohio State University enthusiastically suggested I pursue some research that gave me valuable ideas for this book. Dr. Carol Lyons, also of Ohio State University, graciously read the final manuscript and offered helpful suggestions.

Dr. Dorothy Leal of Ohio University, Dr. Robert Bruinsma of The King's University College, and Dr. Theodore Wade of Gazelle Publications all read early versions of the manuscript and gave valuable advice. So did Dr. Shirley Freed and Dr. James Tucker of Andrews University.

The staff and associates at the Family Literacy Center have faithfully stuck with me during the final editing and reworking of the book. Regina Ruff, Sheila Rice, Julie Davis, and Virginia Ollis offered helpful advice on the manuscript as it proceeded, as did Dr. Carl Smith and Susan Tomlinson. My editor, Ellie Macfarlane, has been the best. She deserves a vacation!

Finally, I want to humbly thank my church family for their support, and especially my Heavenly Father who gave me and my family the grace to see this project through to the end.

Introduction

Nothing else affects a child's future in quite the same way as learning to read. All other schoolwork depends on the ability to read fluently and with understanding. Children who enjoy reading usually get the practice they need to become fluent readers. Their skill in reading makes all the rest of their schoolwork easier. In view of all this, I am sure that you will want your child not only to learn *how* to read but to *enjoy* reading. With your help, your child will realize that reading is not bitter medicine to be swallowed but a gourmet meal to be savored and enjoyed.

I have written this book about teaching a child to read because in my own career I've used and endorsed two very different approaches to reading instruction. For several years, I was headmaster in a school where we used phonics programs in the early grades. I also administered a home education program in which I helped parents who were teaching at home. They, too, used a variety of phonics programs, based on my recommendations. Most of the students learned to read, but many complained about how boring reading was and did not read for enjoyment or enrichment on their own.

Then, in a different setting, I used a book-centered approach that combined reading and writing, in an effort to make reading instruction more enjoyable and meaningful. The children certainly enjoyed books, but some students lacked the specific skills they needed to deal with difficult words and passages. With experience, and further study, I can see the strengths and weaknesses of both approaches.

What I would like to share with you in this book is a way to teach reading that captures the "best of both worlds." I recommend using this method to help a child on the path to literacy. It is an approach that is supported by research and that I have used with great success even with children who have been identified as having difficulty learning to read. In fact, my own son learned to read, almost accidentally, because I shared with him the predictable books that I recommend you use. In addition, my wife and I were doing at home many of the things that I suggest you do to "set the stage" for learning to read. You may read the story of my son in Chapter 4.

In this book, I present to you both the why's and how's of this way of teaching a child to read, following a method that I know from experience to be both enjoyable and effective. Best of all, as you work with your child (or another child you care about), you will be using children's books that you can easily find at your local library—no expensive kits to buy! With this method, you will see how to combine story reading, writing, and an understanding of how to recognize words (phonics) to help your child learn how to read and to enjoy books.

In Appendix A you will find a list of children's books, classified by level of difficulty, so that you will know just which books to use to help your child progress easily from one step to the next. You can take the list to the library and ask the librarian to help you locate the books your child will need next as you work together (you may use those on the list or comparable ones).

I have devoted the first few chapters of this book to the why's of this particular reading method—one that combines phonics with reading children's books and with writing. This part of the book will enable you to understand why the approach works so well. You will learn about the parallels between learning to talk and learning to read, and the importance of reading aloud to your young child. Then you'll find out about what goes on in many of the families of "early readers" (children who learn to read at an early age with no formal instruction) and how you can use some of those practices to help your child. You'll see that there is not a sharp line between readers and nonreaders but rather a gradual progression that your child can make easily and naturally, with your help. In Chapter 4, you will find out what can be learned from a successful early-literacy program for first-graders—techniques that I have adapted for you to use at home.

The "how-to" part of the book starts in Chapter 5. You will find step-by-step guidelines for what you can do to help your child get ready for reading on his own, and how you'll know when he's ready for the next step, and the one after that. There are forms you can copy and use for record-keeping purposes, as well as an entire chapter devoted to a sample lesson that a mother used with her five-year-old child. You will see how to combine reading and writing and word building, all in a single lesson.

I hope that you will enjoy using this book to teach a child to read. Before long, your child will be able to decipher those squiggly black marks on the printed page, and you can welcome him into the "literacy club"—people who enjoy reading. What a marvelous gift to give a child!

CHAPTER 1:
The "Great Debate"

Another book about reading instruction?

Yes, but this one is different. It is written specifically for those who are working one-on-one with a child in a tutoring or home schooling situation. Most manuals written about reading instruction assume that the teacher is working with a classroom full of students. And the reading programs that are designed for individual use recommend a very different approach than the one proposed in this book. What am I talking about?

Consider Janet's story. Not long after Nicole was born, Janet and her husband, Steve, began discussing plans for Nicole's educational future. Because of some strongly held convictions and concerns, home schooling emerged as the option they favored. Janet began collecting and reading all sorts of literature related to teaching children at home. At first, the task of home schooling seemed overwhelming. But as Janet met and talked with other home schooling parents, and as she attended some support group meetings and the state convention, she began to develop a big picture of how to proceed.

The subject area that presented the greatest challenge to both Janet and Steve was reading.

The subject area that presented the greatest challenge to both Janet and Steve was reading. Neither would name reading as a strength . . . both had struggled with learning to read when they were young. Janet had come to realize the importance of being a good role model for Nicole, though, and she had read to Nicole from the first months of her life. Nicole loved sitting with Mom or Dad to enjoy books that they had purchased or checked out from the local library. She seemed to take to it naturally, always asking questions about the pictures, the words in the story, or the underlying message of the text itself. She just couldn't get enough, and her enthusiasm brought a real sense of joy and accomplishment to Steve and Janet. This home schooling thing might turn out to be easier than they had expected!

By the time Nicole was five, she could sing the alphabet song and even name most of the letters individually. Because of Janet's patience in answering questions, Nicole had discovered that some letters stood for certain sounds, like the *n* at the beginning of her name, and the *m* on the McDonald's sign. Both Janet and Steve decided that Nicole was ready to begin a formal reading program.

Their home schooling support group was hosting a curriculum fair the next weekend. Janet was helping to coordinate and run the food booth, but between shifts she looked over the different reading programs on display. Through earlier discussions with other home schoolers who had taught their children to read, Janet was convinced that a phonics approach was the best method to use. As Janet examined the reading materials on display, she soon realized that practically everyone in the home schooling movement felt the same way about phonics. There was little, if anything, available that used any other approach. She chose the program that looked the most colorful and inviting and, though it was somewhat expensive, Janet left the fair with a real sense of anticipation and excitement.

> *Through earlier discussions with other home schoolers who had taught their children to read, Janet was convinced that a phonics approach was the best method to use.*

They started the next Monday morning. Nicole was intrigued with the cute "letter people" characters that were an integral part of the program. She soon was singing along with the cassette tapes, and enjoyed marking her progress along the "reading trail." Janet found the guides to be reasonably easy to follow, and together they proceeded quickly through the simple sounds and blends that made up the first part of the program.

But three weeks into the package, Janet began to notice a change in Nicole's enthusiasm. Nicole would moan when it was reading time, and she acted lethargic and uninterested during the rule recitations and flash card drills.

The only time that Nicole seemed interested in reading was when they shared books together.

Janet's own interest had begun to wane as well; she started to worry that her lack of excitement was rubbing off on Nicole. The only time that Nicole seemed interested in reading was when they shared books together. Janet reflected on how much she and Nicole had enjoyed reading before they had started the program. Maybe they should have just continued what they were doing. What about a more natural approach to teaching reading? Were there any guides available that didn't rely so heavily on drills and memorization? There must be a better (and less expensive) way!

Why this book?

This book will attempt to answer Janet's questions, which, since you've read this far, may be your questions as well. Yours may be a home-schooling family like Janet and Steve's, or you may just want to work more closely with your child as he begins to unlock the secrets of print. Possibly you want to tutor at home or volunteer to help young students who are learning to read at your local school. You may be a college student learning about reading instruction for the first time. Whatever the case, please read on. You will discover some ideas and strategies that have helped to train multitudes of readers who not only *can* read, but who love to read because reading has been exciting and meaningful from their earliest recollections.

The "Great Debate"

There has been much controversy in the world of reading over how instruction should be accomplished. This controversy has continued for more than a century, and in recent writings it has been called "The Great Debate" (Carbo, 1988; Chall, 1989; Turner, 1989). Although there are many facets to the discussion, the core of the debate is whether a phonics approach produces the best readers. By way of definition, a phonics approach, in its purest form, is one in which the student learns the smallest parts of language first, these being letters and their associated sounds. These sounds are then combined to form larger units like blends, digraphs, then syllables, and smaller words. The instruction proceeds to larger units like multisyllable words, then phrases, and finally sentences. Many variations to the approach exist, but all follow similar patterns. A more general term, *bottom-up*, has been given to any approach that starts with the smallest units of language first, as described above.

Although there are many facets to the discussion, the core of the debate is whether a phonics approach produces the best readers.

Another view of reading instruction that uses almost the opposite approach is called *top-down*. Teachers who adhere to a top-down philosophy believe that reading is the process of getting meaning from print, and that reading instruction should remain as whole and natural as possible. Language parts—letters, sounds, phrases, and sentences are dealt with only in the context of whole real language. Teachers who use this book-centered approach believe that, like learning to talk in a "natural" setting, learning to read will occur in the same way if literacy instruction is offered in a whole context without being broken into isolated fragments. Therefore, any type of phonics work is always done in the context of the whole story or piece of writing.

> *The* interactive *model of reading instruction suggests that readers apply both top-down and bottom-up processing . . .*

As is usually true when two groups of people have such strongly held opposing viewpoints, a middle position has been proposed that recognizes elements at both ends of the spectrum. The *interactive* model of reading instruction suggests that readers apply both top-down and bottom-up processing, using information obtained from one process to promote the other. Simply put, a reader uses whatever skills and strategies are in his control to get the message from print. Interactivists believe that if a student knows a great deal about the subject matter, he will not need to use detailed phonics processing to read and comprehend the text. When the student knows little about the topic, he must rely more on the printed word to get the information he needs to understand what he is reading. Therefore, instruction in the reading process should include direct teaching and meaningful practice in both alphabetic coding (phonics) and in the processes of constructing meaning.

The most common form of interactive reading instruction is the basal reading textbook program found in most elementary schools. Basal readers teach many skills such as decoding, comprehension strategies, and vocabulary identification. In many respects, they are more bottom-up in technique, orienting instruction around a prescribed set of increasingly difficult skills. But true bottom-up theorists believe that the common basal program is more top-down because little emphasis is given to pure phonics instruction. Often the phonics instruction in basal reading programs is more general in nature, focusing on groups of words and the similarities in the way they are spelled and pronounced rather than starting with the smallest units of language first.

The most common form of interactive reading instruction is the basal reading textbook program found in most elementary schools.

One method that has received much attention in the last few decades is *sight reading*, also called the *look-say* approach. In look-say, children are taught to read by learning whole words apart from phonetic analysis. The length and shape of each word are key elements in identifying it. Although the look-say approach is used in some basal readers, it is not accepted by everyone. Many who advocate phonics believe this approach has caused a drop in reading scores.

Theorists and educators who hold to each position will argue passionately for their viewpoint. But it is unlikely that any consensus will ever be reached on one best approach to reading instruction. Research continues to be done, and the results suggest that the debate will go on, because each group of theorists can point to past and new research that proves their approach produces superior results. Why is this?

Multiple situations, multiple definitions

When conducting educational research, it is impossible to think about every facet of reading. Many factors are involved in explaining why individuals and groups perform the way they do in different educational settings. Background experience, imparted and acquired attitudes, testing methods, and varying definitions are just a few of the variables that determine success in reading. For example, a phonics curriculum may rely heavily on isolated drill and fill-in-the-blank workbook pages. Students who follow such a curriculum will naturally perform well on standardized tests that contain isolated problems and short-answer questions. What about students who learn to read in classrooms that emphasize books rather than workbook pages? Of course they are at a disadvantage when they have to perform on

But it is unlikely that any consensus will ever be reached on one best approach to reading instruction.

8

standardized tests. In fact, such tests may actually seem disjointed and meaningless to them. The phonics students have been "practicing" all year for the spring achievement tests, but the teacher who uses real literature and materials written by the students as the main teaching tools must either take the time to teach her students how to take the tests, or just hope for the best while continuing to teach in the way she believes is superior. So the question remains, have the phonics students proven that they are better readers? It depends on how you define *better* and exactly what you mean by the term *readers*.

So, the question remains, have the phonics students proven that they are better readers?

What if we asked these students how they define reading and whether they love to read? I'm sure we would get a variety of responses, but my experience has been that most students do not see any difference between instruction and the "real act." To a workbook learner, reading is workbooks. If the student loves workbooks and is successful at filling in the blanks, he will say he loves reading. But what about the little boy who doesn't enjoy endless short-answer exercises and rule recitations? Does he "love to read?" Just ask him sometime. When, in his mind, he pictures workbook pages filled with red correction marks, or when he recalls the embarrassing times that he could not recite the right answer, he will probably look at you with a contorted face that has "Are you kidding?" written all over it. This educational assessment is far more important than grade level equivalencies or percentile points.

Of course there are many phonics-trained children who love to read, as there are many children that are given book-centered instruction who still struggle with their attitudes toward reading. I'm speaking in generalities because of the many factors mentioned above. What is needed is an instructional method that can be tailored to the student's strengths, weaknesses, and preferences so that frustration and waste are avoided. And that is exactly what this book intends to do. Before discussing how to carry out this instructional process, a little more theory should be discussed. Read on!

CHAPTER 2:
Acquiring Language and Learning to Read

Language acquisition

Those educators who follow top-down theories of reading instruction have drawn their inspiration from observing how very young children acquire spoken language. Studies have shown that the process is very similar, no matter which culture or language is observed. What is immediately noticeable about the task of learning to talk is that it is pleasurable and easy for the learner because it is filled with usefulness and meaning. If it weren't for the fact that it has occurred in billions of humans since creation, the thought of a young child so efficiently learning an amazingly complex system in such a short time would seem impossible.

We have all witnessed this process in action. We've all shared in the wonderful joys of watching a little one piece together the complexities of our spoken language. And those of us who have had some measure of responsibility in raising a child from birth have (usually unknowingly) used a very efficient and enjoyable top-down process of instruction to help him or her along. What are the elements of this process that seem to come naturally to both the learner and the teacher? Robert Bruinsma (1990) has nicely summed up the process, and I borrow some of his terminology in my description below.

What is immediately noticeable about the task of learning to talk is that it is pleasurable and easy for the learner because it is filled with usefulness and meaning.

At birth, the child can make a variety of sounds. Early cries and other vocalizations usually bring the comfort the baby needs. Not many months after birth, the child has learned how to get desired results by adjusting the quality and intensity of the noises he makes. Also, the baby begins experimenting with the amazing range of sounds that he can vocalize. This is called the *babbling* stage. Delighted parents babble back to the little one, often insisting that he has said something meaningful in his random play with language. Through this play, the child is learning some very important conventions of language. He is learning about turn-taking that is necessary in meaningful talk. He is also finding out the most important element of language—that it is a meaningful process. The reason that we communicate is to convey some sort of message.

During this stage the child is also listening. He is hearing not just sounds but also the rhythm and pitch elements of speech. Reading to the child in his early months will present the special language elements that are a part of written communication. He will become used to the different rhythms that stories and rhymes in books contain. And just seeing the book and associating it with happy times plants important positive impressions in his soul that are immeasurable.

Reading to the child in his early months will present to him the special language elements that are a part of written communication.

At about twelve months, many children say their first words. These words carry whole messages that the adults around the baby must decipher. For example "bye-bye" may mean "I want to go out now," or it may mean "See you later," or it may mean "Where did my teddy bear go?" The context of the speech is what determines the message. This level of speech development has been called the *holophrastic* or *one-word* stage because whole phrases or sentences are expressed in one word by the child. Rarely do we adults correct the child during this stage of development. Instead, we expand the message by saying "Oh, you want to go away?" or "Yes, I'm leaving now." By these demonstrations we are teaching the child about the way that multiple words express precise meanings.

Let me interject that in this whole process of learning to talk, we almost never drill the child on sounds. We do not isolate sounds or words for the purposes of memorizing them or perfecting them as a prerequisite to use by the child. Drills like this would be *meaningless* to the child because they would be out of context. He might even think that we had somehow regressed to the babbling stage!

We do not isolate sounds or words for the purposes of memorizing them or perfecting them as a prerequisite to use by the child. Drills like this would be meaningless to the child because they would be out of context.

From the age of about 18 months to 30 months the child begins to use short phrases in his speech. Two- and three-word phrases now carry more precise meanings. The language used by the child is similar to the language used in tele-grams, so this phase is sometimes called *telegraphic* speech. The words "Conference over, home Friday" in a telegram means "The conference that I attended is now over. I expect to be home sometime on Friday." When children use telegraphic speech, again the context becomes important because they are not as efficient as adults in concentrating their words. For example, "Hat down" might mean "My hat fell down off the shelf," or "Get my hat down from the hook." Adult responses are again instructive to the child. We naturally ask for clarification or expand on the child's phrase when communicating with him. Much growth in vocabulary occurs during this stage. The average child will have about 50 to 75 words in his vocabulary by the time he reaches 30 months. The more conversations that he has with adults, and the more he is exposed to stories, poems, and rhymes from books, the more his speech capabilities expand.

Being immersed in meaningful language use is the most efficient way to learn the conventions of a language.

An important process that is carried on by the child through language learning is that of *hypothesis testing*. A hypothesis is an educated guess. Whether he is trying to figure out the meaning of a word or how to use the past tense form of a verb, the child will make approximate attempts at using the word in real speech. He judges the appropriateness of his attempt based on the responses he gets from fluent language users. Any sensitive adult will usually confirm the child's use of the word, or, through encouragement, gently adjust the child's attempt by restating what he was trying to express. For example, the child might say "Grandpa, we *goed* to the park!" Grandpa would probably respond, "Oh, you *went* to the park! Did you see any squirrels?" Rarely would Grandpa respond, "Just a minute, son. *Goed* is not a word in the English language. Normally *-ed* is added to the end of a verb to make the past tense form. But the past tense of *go* is *went*, an irregular form. From now on, make sure that you use the correct form." Responding to the child in this way would be absurd because he would not have any meaningful hooks upon which to hang this explanation.

The hypothesis-testing process is going on whenever the child communicates with another person. This is why constant, caring communication is so important to the child's language growth. Being immersed in meaningful language use is the most efficient way to learn the conventions of a language.

Instead of focusing on the missed attempt, we should celebrate the ways that he generalized the rules that govern proper use of the language.

Also, the child should be given much credit when he makes "mistakes" like those in the example above. Instead of focusing on the missed attempt, we should celebrate the ways that he generalized the rules that govern proper use of the language. When the child used the word *goed*, it showed that he had formed a general rule in his mind: when you are talking about something that happened in the past, you add *-ed* to the end of the word that tells what you did. Stop for a moment to think about what the child has pieced together to get to this point. He understands the concept of past and present. He understands which word needed to change form. He substituted the pronoun *we* for all the people, including himself, that went to the park. What an amazing series of accomplishments for a three-year-old child!

This kind of hypothesis testing and rule generating will continue indefinitely, even into adulthood. Any of us use these tools when faced with unfamiliar settings where we need to communicate in new "languages," whether they are foreign dialects or the vocabulary spoken among people in special fields like medicine or computing.

By the time the child is 10, he has fine-tuned his basic use of the language. He may have a vocabulary of between 3,000 to 40,000 words depending on his exposure to conversation with fluent adults and on the amount and variety of reading he has done. During this time, formal literacy training can meaningfully take place because the child realizes that language is a thing that can be looked at and talked about. Now it would be benefi-cial to discuss verb tenses and parts of speech and expect the child to apply these rules to his own use of language.

This kind of hypoth-esis testing and rule generating will continue indefinitely, even into adulthood.

The overriding theme that I want to convey through the above discussion is that, as a child learns to talk, we are not instructing the child through traditional means like those found in grade school. We are not depending on someone's interpretation and prescription of a sequenced set of skills to teach the child how to talk before allowing him to engage in actual speech. The "natural" methods that humans ap-pear to have been gifted with by the Creator are amazingly efficient and enjoyable for both the learner and the teacher. Why should learning to read be any different?

Learning to read and write is related to oral language learning

Recent research that has looked at literacy learning from a child's point of view has given us new insights into how young children learn to read and write (Strickland, 1990). Some of these insights, which are held to be true by most early childhood experts, are expressed below:

◆ **Learning to read and write begins early in life and is ongoing.** When a child's environment is filled with meaningful print, he is constantly observing and learning about written language.

◆ **Learning to read and write are interrelated processes that develop together with learning to talk.** Children do not see the differences in reading, writing, and talking that we adults see. In the right environment, reading and writing can develop as naturally as talking.

◆ **Learning to read and write requires active participation in activities that have meaning in a child's daily life.** Letter writing and list making, when done with the child, can be more instructional and meaningful than any drill exercise could ever hope to be.

◆ **Learning to read and write involves interaction with responsive others.** Just as in learning to talk, it is the relationships with loved ones and caregivers that add a depth of meaning to reading and writing experiences. The joy found in those relationships enhances the pleasure of reading and writing together.

◆ **Learning to read and write is particularly enhanced by shared book experiences.** Family storybook reading plays a unique role in a young child's literacy development. No other single activity has as much potential instructional value for both attitudinal and academic enrichment.

Concerns about packaged phonics programs

Contrast all of the above with the approach in a rigid phonics program. The view that it makes sense to assemble literacy by piecing together the smallest parts of print into bigger and bigger pieces only makes sense in an adult's mind. Children, who naturally strive to make meaning out of each experience in life, may easily be confused by such a fragmented approach. It is my opinion that the children who successfully learn to read with a rigid phonics program can do so only because many meaningful foundations of literacy were already in place.

In an incisive article titled "Beware of 'Magic' Phonics Programs," Professors William Anderson and Ann Fordham (Anderson, 1991) express seven concerns they have with "quick-fix" phonics reading programs:

◆ **Phonics programs are potentially boring and may lead to a dislike of reading.** Catchy tunes soon lose their appeal, as does the charm of the puppets or race tracks. Drill is drill, no matter how it is disguised.

◆ **Phonics programs may misrepresent what reading is.** Being a competent reader requires more than just memorizing a tape. Many more strategies are involved in being a fluent reader, and these are best learned using real literature, not production line programs.

◆ **Phonics programs cost money that would be better spent on books.** The authors calculate that parents could purchase at least 30 paperback books and also subscribe to a children's magazine for less money than the most widely publicized commercial phonics program costs.

◆ **Phonics programs may lead to unrealistic expectations for children.** Parents may erroneously conclude that their child is learning disabled if he does not make the magic gains promised by these programs. The child may not be able to learn successfully using this presentation mode, or he may simply be bored with the materials.

◆ **Phonics programs ignore realities of development in acquiring mastery of print.** Children develop at different rates in their understanding of print. These programs do little to take differences into account. To believe that one phonics package can work equally well with all children is a fallacy.

◆ **Phonics programs use time that would be better spent in reading aloud together.** The value of reading aloud cannot be overemphasized. The highly respected national report, *Becoming a Nation of Readers*, identifies reading aloud as "the single most important activity for building the knowledge required for eventual success in reading." (Anderson 1985, p. 23).

◆ **Phonics programs overlook the fact that knowledge gained by rote memory does not readily apply to the complexities of actual reading.** The shallow learning from persistent drill programs does not automatically guarantee a child's success with real print in real literature.

Knowledge of letters and their corresponding sounds is incredibly important, but my concern is for how children are taught this awareness. I propose that formal literacy instruction should continue and enhance the processes that have worked so well for the child since birth. In the next chapter, we will begin looking more specifically at the characteristics of a natural, language-centered approach to literacy instruction.

In summary

The following chart, adapted from *What's Whole in Whole Language?* by Ken Goodman (1986) may help to sum up what has been said in this chapter. Take some time to meditate on its message.

What Makes Language Very Easy or Very Hard to Learn?

It's *Easy* When:	It's *Hard* When:
It's real and natural.	It's artificial.
It's whole.	It's broken into tiny pieces.
It's sensible.	It's nonsense.
It's interesting.	It's dull and uninteresting.
It's relevant.	It's irrelevant to the learner.
It belongs to the learner.	It belongs to somebody else.
It's part of a real event.	It's out of context.
It has social utility.	It has no social value.
It has purpose for the learner.	It has no discernible purpose.
It's accessible to the learner.	It's inaccessible.
The learner chooses to use it.	It's imposed by someone else.
The learner has the power.	The learner is powerless to use it.

CHAPTER 3:
Early Readers: What Can They Teach Us?

Early readers: What can we learn from them?

Several research studies in the last 30 years have looked into the phenomenon of early readers (Thomas, 1985). Early readers are children who, with no formal instruction, can read reasonably well at the ages of three, four, or five. By looking at these children and their home environments, researchers have tried to piece together common elements that have contributed to their unusual achievements.

One point that needs to be made early in this discussion is that, although these children received no *formal* instruction in reading, this does not mean that their parents or caregivers were not involved or instrumental in their learning to read. Quite the contrary. Research on early readers has discovered a number of common factors, and almost all of them relate to the adults in a child's life. Early readers were read to frequently by parents and other adults or older siblings. The parents of early readers were avid readers themselves. Thus, they served as important models for reading behavior, and this helped to identify and define reading processes for their children. Early readers usually had abundant access to age-appropriate reading materials. These books and magazines were both owned by the children and checked out from the local library. But these factors alone did not lead to a child's becoming an early reader. What else contributed to their early successes with print?

Language and reading acquisition parallels

Often unknowingly, the parents of early readers used many similar or parallel processes identified in the previous chapter on language acquisition. One interesting common characteristic noted in early-reading children is that their ability to speak was more developed when compared to nonreading children of similar age, IQ, and social status. This may be because these children had a natural aptitude for language, but it is more likely that they began speaking early because they had many opportunities to talk to adults and older children. Early-reading children spent much time in the company of people who were talking with them and with each other. These people would speak with the children in adult-like ways, and they supported the children's attempts to converse with them. Often, baby-talking to these children was not tolerated by their guardians. Because of this, these early-reading children developed mature speaking habits early in their lives, and many researchers even noted a heightened use of more poetic and metaphoric language.

Early-reading children spent much time in the company of people who were talking with them and with each other.

Let's get specific about the processes used by parents in helping their children learn to talk. Sensitive adults will answer all the questions asked or implied by children about elements of our language. Most parents who pay attention to their children will continue the topics introduced by them, thereby adding to their understanding of our language. They also add new information to their children's utterances. It appears that the more importance that parents place on these responses, the more rapidly their children's language use develops. Perhaps an example would be helpful.

Suppose that three-year-old Mary is looking out the window. She asks her mother, "Is the sun burny today?" Mother lays aside the checkbook she was balancing, goes to the window, and says, "Yes, it is very hot today, and the sun is bright. If we went outside and sat in the sun for too long, we would get burned." Notice how Mother answered the question and expanded on it. She did not correct her child's use of language, although at times it would be appropriate and helpful to do so. Mary's perceptions about the current conditions outside and her knowledge of how to express her perceptions were fine-tuned just a little more by this exchange. The more often she engages in such conversations with adults, the more her own language and general knowledge will develop.

Most parents who pay attention to their children will continue the topics introduced by them, thereby adding to their understanding of our language.

Adults often provide support by responding to children in ways that take the risk out of their attempts to use the language they are still struggling to learn. Because of the support of those around them, young children are not afraid to keep testing their hypotheses about how to use words or how to structure a sentence. Their adult "teachers" conceal their concern or amusement about the child's misuse of language and respond to his or her message instead. Any correction is disguised in their response. In the conversation between Mary and Mother above, Mother seemed to delight in her child's creative use of the nonword *burny*. She responded directly to what Mary meant by her question, and she corrected her use of the word *burn* in a nonthreatening way. A negative response about the wrong use of the word might have put an end to the conversation and to any subsequent learning as well. Too much correction would eventually lead Mary to believe that it is better not to try at all.

Adults often provide support by responding to children in ways that take the risk out of their attempts to use the language they are still struggling to learn.

A conscientious parent requires the child to be accountable for the particular aspects of language he has mastered. Refusing to accept deliberate baby talk is one example of this accountability. In addition, a parent can gently insist that the child answer a particular question if the parent is aware that the child already knows the answer. This ensures that the child does not lose through misuse or nonuse what he has already mastered.

The processes described above were used (often unknowingly) by the parents of early readers as their children learned to talk *and* as they learned to read. Let's examine the same processes as they apply to early literacy instruction.

When interviewed, the parents, grandparents, and older siblings of early readers said that they answered all questions of these early readers regarding print, pictures, and text. Rarely did they refuse a request by the child to sit together and read a book. In fact, early readers were read to more times within a day than comparable nonreaders. It appears that the sheer quantity of experience with the printed word contributed greatly to their early fluency with text. The fact that they were not often turned down in their requests to read may have relayed the message that reading is a valuable and enjoyable pursuit.

It appears that the sheer quantity of experience with the printed word contributed greatly to their early fluency with text.

Parents of early readers frequently reported that their children had memorized stories or books. This accomplishment may be a very important clue to early fluency in reading. Possibly the child has discovered that the print records the story exactly, and the story can be repeated exactly each time it is read. This may then lead to the realization that the print is like a code that can be deciphered, even by a person like himself! So the child may begin searching for patterns in print that would help him to read new stories on his own.

The number of fluent language users that worked with the child was important only as it related to the frequency of interactions that the child had each day. What was more important than the number of people involved with the child was the quality of these interactions on a regular basis. Making the most out of each experience with print by answering all of the child's questions, and even taking them one step further, contributed to early success in reading.

Early readers probably enjoyed these regular reading experiences because they were both pleasurable and non-threatening. The children were successful in whatever was asked of them during their read-aloud sessions because the adults with whom they read structured it this way. If the child tried to read a page on his own, any attempt was praised and gently readjusted if necessary.

Parents of early readers would ask questions about the book before, during, and after the reading. These questions would help the child glean the message from the story because they would set the stage so the child would know better what to expect. As the child matured in this read-aloud questioning process, most of the parents noted that the questioning burden began to shift more to the child. He began to show that he was, in his mind, becoming responsible for comprehending and assessing the message of the book. The parent would then become a trusted resource to whom the child could turn.

Early readers probably enjoyed these regular reading experiences because they were both pleasurable and nonthreatening.

Because of the support they received, early readers rarely had to be coaxed into any task involving books or print. These children began to see reading as their responsibility. Sensitive parents fostered this responsibility by answering the child's call to read a story or play a word game whenever possible. They always expressed delight whenever their children could "read" a new book or identify a new word out of context. They held the children responsible for the knowledge they had already gained. Identifying letters on a keyboard, naming individual words on word cards, or insisting that the child point to words that he knows in a book are all examples of this accountability in practice.

The magic key: Reading aloud

The most important activity for building the knowledge and skills eventually required for reading is that of reading aloud to children. In this, both the sheer amount of and the choice of reading materials seems to make a difference. (Adams, 1990, p. 86)

This quote by reading expert Marilyn Adams (from whom we will hear more later) reflects the consensus of all informed reading educators. On the preceding pages we have seen that reading aloud by parents contributed the most to the child's early language development. It is in the context of experiencing good literature together that a child is introduced to all of the enjoyable and important elements in reading.

It is in the context of experiencing good literature together that a child is introduced to all of the enjoyable and important elements in reading.

In one study designed to determine if early talkers necessarily become early readers, the researchers made some surprising discoveries (Crain-Thorenson, 1992). Only one of the 25 early-talking children observed actually was demonstrating advanced reading at age 4½. As part of the study, the researchers also monitored the amount of story reading in the homes of these children, as well as the amount of instruction in letter names and sounds in preschool years that they received. The phonics instruction given to the children did play a role in their later literacy and language development. But storybook reading by parents was found to be a significantly more important factor in their children's becoming readers. One notable conclusion from the study suggested that "story reading with parents is fueling the growth of knowledge at the 'leading edge' of the child's development."

The recognized expert in the read-aloud movement is Jim Trelease, author of *The Read-Aloud Handbook* (Trelease, 1995). I wholeheartedly recommend his book, multiple copies of which are available in the juvenile department of most public libraries. He provides a list of recommendations for parents or teachers as they read aloud to their children. I will provide an edited list based on his suggestions for you to consider as a parent.

Read-aloud suggestions:

◆ *Begin reading to children as soon as possible.* The younger, the better.

◆ *Read as often as possible.*

◆ *Try to set aside at least one traditional time each day for a story.* Trelease recommends both bedtime and before the kids leave for school each morning.

◆ *Start with picture books and build to storybooks or novels.*

◆ *Be patient as you cultivate the art of listening in your young child.*

◆ *Don't continue reading a book once it is obvious it was a poor choice.*
Read only books that you and your child enjoy.

◆ *Vary the length and subject matter of your readings.* Trelease especially recommends Mother Goose rhymes and songs for infants to stimulate language and listening.

◆ *Occasionally read above your child's intellectual level, but not above his emotional level.*

◆ *Allow time for discussion before and after the reading session.* Don't become impatient with questions. Foster the child's curiosity and his initiatives in learning about print.

◆ *Use plenty of expression when reading.* Change your tone at appropriate times, or read slowly during suspenseful parts.

◆ *Try to find out more about the author.* Books are written by people, not machines. Talk together about the author's unique style, etc.

◆ *Arrange for time each day for the child to read by himself, even if the child's "reading" is turning the pages and looking at the pictures.*

◆ *Lead by example.* Make sure your child sees you reading for pleasure during times other than read-aloud.

Learning letter names and their sounds

I will talk later about specific methods to teach children about the letters in words and the phonetic generalizations that accompany them. But some comments should be made concerning the informal ways children learn the alphabet as they share reading and writing experiences with the adults in their lives.

Most children who have been read to regularly by responsive, caring parents will gain much knowledge about letters as a natural by-product, especially if questioning is encouraged and responded to warmly.

Most children who have been read to regularly by responsive, caring parents will gain much knowledge about letters as a natural by-product, especially if questioning is encouraged and responded to warmly. In addition, writing with and in front of the child will expose him to valuable insights regarding the uses for written language and the conventions we utilize when we write. It is important for the adult to carefully explain what he or she is doing and why, and to answer every question the child may ask about writing and the printed word.

Look for opportunities to write with the child for many purposes. Keeping an informal diary or journal, writing letters to Grandma or other loved ones, or writing out a shopping list are very valuable activities that will help the child to learn much about letters and sounds.

Perhaps one of the single most instructive activities in which you and your child could participate is in writing short stories together. Allow the child to dictate the story to you as you write down his words. It's fine to correct his language as you write as long as it is not done in a discouraging way. Say each word slowly, sound the letters or letter blends as you write, and then spell the word back before going to the next word. Frequently repeat the sentence as you are completing it so the child (and you) don't forget what you are writing. Read each sentence as it is finished, pointing to each word as you read. When you are finished with the story, allow the child to illustrate it, or work together to add some special "pizzazz." You will find that, with practice, the child will be able to read the story himself. Encourage him by suggesting that he read the story to any interested person that comes to visit.

Some cautions . . .

The following appeared recently in *Focus On the Family* magazine in the section titled "Dr. Dobson answers your questions." I wholeheartedly agree with Dr. Dobson's recommendations:

Q. I've read that it's possible to teach 4-year-olds to read. Should I be working on this with my child?

A. If a youngster is particularly sharp and can learn to read without feeling undue adult pressure, it might be advantageous to teach him this skill. But that's a much bigger "if" than most people realize. Few parents can work with their own children without showing frustration over natural failures.

The best policy is to provide your children with many interesting books and materials, read to them and answer their questions. Then let nature take its unobstructed course (Dobson, 1995).

In this chapter I have described common characteristics of the environmental conditions found in the homes and lives of early readers. I have also suggested ways that you can use these insights in carrying out your own informal read-aloud and writing program. I am not describing a rigid program that you need to begin in your home, nor am I suggesting that your child needs to be forced to fit a particular mold. I am simply offering some observations that may be instructional to you as you prepare to teach your child to read. If he does not read on his own at the age of five or six, even though most of the optimum factors are present, don't panic! Anxiety about a perceived lack of progress will do more to harm than help your child in the pursuit of literacy.

Parents should abandon the mentality that would cause them to try to raise a superbaby. There is no inherent value in trying to teach a child to read at the age of three unless he is some sort of rare genius whose growth would be thwarted by holding him back. Most of us parents need not concern ourselves with this kind of situation because we don't have this kind of child. Striving to create a child prodigy can only cause undue social and emotional stress.

I like to use the analogy of growing a beautiful rose to illustrate my motivation for discussing early readers. A wise gardener would discover what the optimum conditions were for growing a prizewinning rose. He would plant it in the perfect soil that had just the right amount of acidity. He would expose it to just the right amount of sunshine. He would water it at just the right time of day. He would feed it with the perfect balance of nutrients. He would gently remove any weeds that threatened to choke the rose, or that would compete with it for water and minerals. Then he would sit back and, maybe with a prayer, let God and nature take their course. And when that first bud appeared, never would he try to force it open. May we take the same tack in growing our little readers.

The following list of dos and don'ts will help to guide you in growing a young reader.

Growing a Young Reader

Do:

- ◆ Provide an atmosphere rich in print.
- ◆ Read aloud with the child as often as possible, at least daily.
- ◆ Be a reading role model for your child.
- ◆ Delight in interactions about print with your child.
- ◆ Look for opportunities to write with your child.
- ◆ Respond as often as possible to your child's initiatives.
- ◆ Gently adjust your child's mistakes by modeling correct usage.
- ◆ Use plenty of encouragement.
- ◆ Ask and solicit lots of questions.
- ◆ Appropriately hold the child accountable for what s/he knows.

Don't:

- ◆ Criticize the child or his/her attempts.
- ◆ Deny the child too often when s/he requests reading activities.
- ◆ Point out every mistake.
- ◆ Allow the child to deliberately baby talk or act in an immature way.
- ◆ Try to raise a child prodigy by pressuring.
- ◆ Expect more than is reasonable.

CHAPTER 4:
What Works? One Successful Program

The "Great Debate" revisited

Many people have looked deeply into all aspects of reading instruction by doing all types of research. Volumes have been written about the pros and cons of every approach. Instead of laboring through an intensive synopsis of current thought, let me say that there is adequate positive material to warrant a literature-based approach to reading instruction (Tunnell, 1989). The philosophy has been implemented by many different people in many different situations, and it has borne enough verifiable positive fruit to justify its continued use and development.

There is also an abundance of research to warrant certain aspects of a phonics approach to reading instruction. The now famous report by the National Institute of Education titled *Becoming a Nation of Readers* (Anderson, 1985) forcefully asserted that direct instruction in alphabetic coding helps children learn to read.

. . . an increasing number of experts recommend an approach that integrates all elements of the reading process.

In an article titled "Romance and Reality" (Stanovich, 1994), Dr. Keith Stanovich dives headlong into the reading debate armed with his own research findings and the findings of others. He proposes a five-step strategy for resolving, or at least quieting, the dispute over how best to teach reading. The crux of his proposal involves looking for areas of agreement, identifying crucial differences, deciding if the differences are worth the cost of "war," and then letting further research determine the truth. Stanovich, along with other persons knowledgeable in the field, believes that the differences are not that great. Several key elements of a language- and literature-centered approach have been acknowledged as valuable by reading experts on both sides of the debate. They have to do with the benefits of integrating reading and writing, child-centered instruction, and teacher empowerment (vs. mindlessly following curriculum guides). There is more disagreement over the actual form that phonics instruction ought to take, and whether phonetic knowledge can be acquired by all children as naturally as spoken language is.

No knowledgeable reading teacher would say that deliberate instruction in phonics principles is harmful to young readers. The debate is over how it is accomplished and in what contexts. Few, if any, of the leading voices in the debate recommend teaching phonics in a vacuum. Programs that simply start out by drilling students in sounds and rules are not considered exemplary by even the staunchest phonics advocates—or at least those who base their views on current research. Instead, an increasing number of experts recommend an approach that integrates all elements of the reading process. These elements include both reading and listening to real, quality literature, writing in conjunction with reading, and phonics being taught *explicitly* in the context of the above.

To see how these lofty objectives can be accomplished in real life, let's turn our focus to one successful reading program whose development has been both guided and verified by much field-based research.

Reading Recovery®*

Reading Recovery is an early-intervention reading program designed to help at-risk first graders become proficient at reading before they fall hopelessly behind. Designed by New Zealand child psychologist Marie Clay, the program

The name Reading Recovery® is a registered trademark of the Reading Recovery Program and may not be used without permission of the Ohio State University.

was developed after years of observation and research. Clay and her colleagues watched good readers closely to discover what strategies they used in their early stages of learning to read. They also observed, through a one-way glass, teachers tutoring children as they learned to read. As they watched, they discussed pupil and teacher responses. After the session, they would challenge the teachers who had demonstrated to explain why they had chosen specific techniques, books, or instructional progressions. According to Clay in her first guidebook, *The Early Detection of Reading Difficulties (1979)*,

Reading Recovery is an early-intervention reading program designed to help at-risk first graders become proficient at reading before they fall hopelessly behind.

> *A large number of techniques were piloted, observed, discussed, argued over, related to theory, analyzed, written up, modified and tried out in various ways, and, most important, many were discarded. Carefully graded sequences within each technique were described. Thus the procedures were derived from the responses of experienced teachers to children as they tried to read and write. The process of refinement continued over the next three years, as several drafts of the teaching procedures were written, discussed and edited by the teachers. The procedures were derived from the practice of teachers who were working with failing children but they were discussed and analyzed in relation to current theories of the reading process. (p. 84)*

The resulting program was first field tested and implemented in New Zealand and then in Columbus, Ohio, with very favorable results. Since then, Reading Recovery has been implemented in many school systems all over the United States, New Zealand, Australia, Canada, and the United Kingdom.

Only the lowest 20% of first grade children are admitted into the program. Those who are discontinued from the program—approximately three-fourths of those admitted—receive an average of 65–70 half-hour tutoring sessions from a trained Reading Recovery teacher. Before a child is discontinued, she must be reading at the average level of her classmates, and she must be using a self-improving set of reading strategies regularly. More than 75% of these children, in most studies, continue to improve in reading along with their classmates, with no further remediation needed. This is extraordinary, considering that these were the students who displayed the least proficiency in reading in first grade.

. . . Reading Recovery has been implemented in many school systems all over the United States, Australia, and Canada.

Each year, many statistical reports are filed by those who administer the Reading Recovery program in their respective training sites. The results continue to be outstanding. No other reading program can boast this kind of success, whether it is a phonics program, a textbook program, or otherwise. (Swartz & Klein, 1997)

Several years ago, I had the opportunity to carry out my own research project examining the continuing progress of Reading Recovery graduates in our district. The program was in its third year of implementation, so I tested the second and third grade students who had graduated from the program in the first grade. I found that only 45% of these students scored within the average range when looking at their scores on the California Achievement Test (CAT). I was not surprised because, like all achievement tests, this test breaks reading up into a series of subskills that are somewhat unrelated to *real* reading. Reading Recovery students are not trained to read this way. When I tested these students and a random sampling of non-Reading Recovery students using a text reading level (TRL) test, I got very different results. The TRL test uses a series of graded reading passages. The student reads the passage orally as the administrator keeps a record of miscues (mistakes) made by the student. When a student scores below 90% accuracy on two consecutive levels, the testing is stopped. The student's reading level is defined as the highest level at which she read at 90% or better accuracy. When compared to the nonprogram children using the TRL test, just under 80% of the program students scored within the average range of their classmates. Even more remarkably, 45% of the second grade program children scored *above* the average range. Remember, these students were ranked in the lowest 20% when compared to their first-grade classmates!

The goal of Reading Recovery is to help each child make the greatest gains in reading in the shortest time possible.

Though some children do not "graduate" from the program in the time allotted, they still make greater progress in reading than if they had not been enrolled. I recall one little boy named Timmy, with whom I worked. He entered the program and, although his progress was not remarkable, it was consistent. His feelings of self-worth grew immensely because of his experience in this kind of setting. I acknowledged and celebrated any progress that he made. Every day he went home with a book that he could read. It became necessary to remove him from the program before discontinuing because he was identified as developmentally handicapped by the school psychologist. State regulations prohibited allowing him to be served by more than one special program at a time. During a discussion that I had with the psychologist about Timmy, she noted some remarkable inconsistencies in Timmy's tests. He scored more than two years behind his chronological age in all subject areas except reading and writing. He was near his age-mates in these areas even though, according to his IQ scores, he shouldn't have been. She gave all the credit to his few weeks in the Reading Recovery program.

The goal of Reading Recovery is to help each child make the greatest gains in reading in the shortest time possible. The time factor is important for several reasons. First, quickly accelerating and discontinuing students allows more needy children to be served. Since it is a one-on-one instructional program, it is fairly expensive to operate when using a student-to-teacher cost-analysis ratio. And most important, the sooner a child is helped, the less likely he is to develop bad habits that are hard to break.

What the experts say about Reading Recovery

Not surprisingly, Reading Recovery has drawn praise from many sectors. Dr. Glen Robinson is the Director of Research at the Educational Research Service in Arlington, Virginia. The ERS is an independent, nonprofit organization providing research and information for school decision makers. In the foreword for the ERS monograph *Reading Recovery: Early Intervention for At-Risk First Graders* (Pinnel, 1988), he states, "Although the Educational Research Service, in accordance with its standard policy, does not endorse any particular program or instructional method, the Reading Recovery results and evaluations presented in this manuscript deserve special consideration of educators and concerned citizens nationwide."

. . . Reading Recovery results . . . deserve special consideration of educators and concerned citizens nationwide.

Even more notable is the recommendation given by researcher Marilyn Adams, author of the book *Beginning To Read: Thinking and Learning About Print* (1990). She wrote the book under contract with the federally funded Center for the Study of Reading at the University of Illinois. Its purpose was to help resolve the dispute between the proponents of phonics and the proponents of book-centered instructional approaches. She concludes at the end of her 600-page report that elements of both philosophies are necessary in a well-balanced reading program. So much for resolving the debate! But what is remarkable is the exemplary status given to the Reading Recovery program. She cites it as one of the best examples of both approaches in action, and that all students should have this kind of balanced instruction in learning to read!

Reading Recovery has all of the elements of a well-rounded reading instruction program. Most phonics instruction is done within the context of reading and writing about real stories in real books. There is no set sequence of sounds or rules that must be taught precept upon precept. Relatively little isolated drill occurs. The needs of the student determine each day's progression of instruction. Students learn a set of strategies that help them to become self-improving readers. And yet Dr. Adams believes that its approach is exemplary in teaching knowledge about phonics. How does the program work?

The basic elements of the Reading Recovery approach

The student is first given an observation survey test (Clay, 1993a) intended to gauge his knowledge about letters, words, and print, his reading comprehension abilities, and his writing skills. The teacher writes a plan of instructional goals for the child that guides her in her work with the child. The next two weeks are spent in a time called "roaming around the known." During each day's half-hour session the teacher and the student informally share books and writing activities together. The teacher is making further observations, seeking to know more about the child's unique strengths and weaknesses. When formal lessons begin, the child is introduced to a new book each day that is right on the "cutting edge" of his abilities. He also does some rereading of familiar books, one of which is evaluated for accuracy by the teacher. Each day the child writes a sentence about a book he has read or a personal experience. During this time, much work is done with letters, sounds, and word identification. When the teacher thinks that the child has made significant progress, demonstrating that he has developed a set of self-improving reading strategies, he is tested to verify his progress. If the child tests out at the average reading level in his class, he is discontinued from the one-on-one tutoring program.

A closer look at a Reading Recovery lesson

Every Reading Recovery lesson is different for every child because each lesson includes choices made by the child during the lesson. The instruction focuses on that child's strengths and weaknesses as revealed previously *and* during that particular lesson. However, a typical Reading Recovery lesson has the following basic format:

1. **Familiar Rereading**—The child selects and reads two or three short books (or a portion of a longer book) which he has read previously with 90-100% accuracy. The teacher centers instruction around a few of the strengths and weaknesses exhibited, primarily those which pertain to that lesson's focus of instruction (as determined by an analysis of the previous lesson).

2. **Running Record**—The child reads the book introduced the previous day without intervention except in extreme cases. The teacher makes a running record (a shorthand way to record the child's reading), reacting to his reading and making a few teaching points only after the selection has been completed.

3. **Letter Identification/word making and breaking**—Most letter work is done in the context of the child's reading and writing; however, this portion of the lesson may be included if the child can recognize only a few letters (usually less than ten). One or two letters are taught and practiced for a maximum of two to three minutes.

   As the child gains mastery over letter identification, the focus of this lesson component shifts to constructing and reconstructing words that illustrate basic phonics principles. Often, the words are taken from something the child has just read. The teacher uses the chalkboard, magnetic letters, a dry erase board, or paper and pencil, to work with words.

4. **Writing**—The child dictates and writes a short story (often a single sentence) with teacher assistance as required. The child then reassembles a cut-up version of that story. Instruction focuses on the development of strategies for writing unknown words and fluent writing of high-frequency words.

5. **New Book**—A new book, selected to accelerate learning on the basis of an analysis of the previous lesson, is introduced by the teacher and then attempted by the child. This book will be the next day's running record book.

The typical lesson described above takes about 30 minutes. The teacher has been trained how to respond most effectively to the difficulties that her students may encounter. Instruction is very "efficient"—the teacher does not labor long on any one problem. All teaching and discussion are very positive and encouraging. The child always leaves the lesson with a book to share at home and with a sense of accomplishment because of the new things he learned that day.

What can we learn from Reading Recovery?

Reading Recovery teachers receive intense training during their first year in the program. At the beginning of each weekly training session, they watch one of their peers teach an actual lesson to a student through a one-way mirror. Three times during that year, each teacher has herself been under scrutiny behind the glass. During the teaching session and afterward, the rest of the teachers-in-training discuss the method used and the choices made by the teacher being observed. They frequently challenge her decisions, but also offer praise for exemplary teaching. All of this is overseen and directed by a trained teacher leader who has been through this process many times.

This training is an important key to the success of the program. But remember the unique situation faced by Reading Recovery teachers. They must help each child make accelerated progress in learning to read and write. They work only with children who are severely at-risk. They work within very limited time-frames. Parents teaching their children at home or school volunteers are usually not faced with such restrictive demands.

The primary keys to the success of the Reading Recovery program are the methods used, many of which have been around for a long time. They are not difficult to learn, and they reflect the more "natural" processes already described in the previous chapter. Remember, a child who has had the types of positive experiences already described would more than likely not qualify for the Reading Recovery program. He has already had the most important foundations for reading laid in his life, foundations that are usually missing for severely at-risk children.

A personal testimony

My second son, Jeffrey, was three years old during my training year in Reading Recovery. Through many informal read-aloud sessions, he had been exposed to books and print. He knew a few letters, but he did not know any of their sounds. I'm not sure he knew, at that time, how to write his name.

Jeffrey commented, "Remember when we used to read all those little books and you made me point with my finger? That's when I learned to read."

I would frequently bring home some of the little books (predictable easy readers) that are an important part of the program. We would sit together and, without presenting a formal lesson, read the books. I would have him read after me, showing him how to point at the words as he read. Because of the predictable and repetitive nature of these books, he could "read" each one after only five or ten minutes. Of course, Jeffrey would read his books to everyone who walked in the door. I would bring home progressively more difficult books and introduce them to Jeffrey who would, in turn, read them over and over.

During that next summer, I was offered a job teaching sixth grade in our local school. I no longer had access to the books I used in Reading Recovery, but my wife, my mother, and I all continued a normal read-aloud program at home. Jeffrey continued to learn about print and reading. He knew many letters, sounds, and words, and he was familiar with basic knowledge about books and stories.

When Jeffrey was six, he entered kindergarten at the school where I taught. Before the end of that year, he was reading simple books even with no previous introduction. I marveled at how quickly he progressed in his reading because our kindergarten program does not include formal reading instruction.

One evening as we were reading together, I commented on how pleased I was with Jeffrey's progress. I praised his teacher for doing such a good job teaching him to read. Jeffrey became exasperated and said, "She didn't teach me to read. You did!"

Any good reader can teach someone else to read with a little guidance. You need not invest great amounts of time and money . . .

I was surprised, so I asked him, "When did I teach you to read?"

Jeffrey commented, "Remember when we used to read all those little books and you made me point with my finger? That's when I learned to read. Mrs. Thomas [his kindergarten teacher] just taught me a bunch of animals and stuff" [referring to the letter-learning program she uses]. In his mind, he equated learning to read with the simple predictable books that should be a part of every early literacy program.

The teaching methods that I propose in this book are based on natural procedures that are a part of every literate family's routine life. But many of the specific techniques are patterned after those used in literature-based classrooms and in successful programs like Reading Recovery.

Any good reader can teach someone else to read with a little guidance. You need not invest great amounts of time and money in a precisely engineered program like those commonly found on the market. You just need to know how to discover your child's unique abilities and needs and, through the medium of good literature, lead him to an understanding and appreciation of the printed word.

CHAPTER 5:
Using "Real Books" in Your Program

Books: The core of a good reading program

The statement that books should be the central, most important element in any reading program may, at first, seem self-evident. But, as I've already mentioned, my review of tutoring and home education resources has revealed that most reading curricula do not introduce real books into the program right at the beginning. Letter cards, memorization drills, and the like are the primary modes of instruction in the first months of these programs. Any stories that are used are ones that are usually devised to meet some phonetic purpose.

Most of these stories use language that is unnatural and, therefore, unfamiliar to young readers. The sentences often sound choppy and may be hard for a child to read fluently. The following example, taken from the intensive phonics-based manual *How to Tutor* by Samuel Blumenfeld (1973, p. 49), will serve to illustrate this point:

> **Dan has an ax.**
> **Has Dan an ax?**
> **Sam has ham.**
> **Has Sam ham?**
> **Dan has land and sand.**
> **Has Dan sand?**
> **Sam sat.**
> **Dan sat.**

Obviously, the above example was contrived by Blumenfeld to help the student practice the short *a* sound. Proponents of skill-based programs would be quick to point out that these drills are not intended for meaning or enjoyment. They have a specific purpose, and that is to provide practice in a particular element of their reading skills sequence. Blumenfeld, on page 43 of *How to Tutor*, states "Emphasis on comprehension and meaning should not begin until *after* [emphasis his] the child has mastered the entire sound-symbol system and can read and write with ease every word in his own speaking vocabulary."

I'm not sure that many children are able to separate practice from the real thing, nor should they be expected to. We did not prevent them from talking with us until they had mastered every sound in our language, and until they had a speaking vocabulary of at least 400 words! Learning to read, like learning to talk, can and ought to be meaningful and enjoyable from the start.

The writers of many phonics programs instinctively realize that the process should be enjoyable and not boring. This is why they introduce all sorts of artificial elements into their programs to make them fun—elements like puppets, songs, letter people, rewards, and colorful progress charts. Since repetitive drill and contrived stories are things that most children would soon learn to dislike, they must be supplemented with rewards, games, and songs to keep the students interested. Therefore, the focus is taken away from reading for real purposes. When the child thinks "reading," he thinks "games" or "songs" or "toys" or "drills" or "boring."

A reading program that uses real children's literature as the primary instructional tool has purposefulness and enjoyment built right into it.

A reading program that uses real children's literature as the primary instructional tool has purposefulness and enjoyment built right into it. After all, children's books are meant to be enjoyed. Otherwise they would not have been written and published. Learning to read with real books delivers its own rewards as a part of the process. Contrast the selection from *How to Tutor* with the following selection from *Brown Bear, Brown Bear* (1984) by Bill Martin:

Brown bear, brown bear, what do you see?
I see a redbird looking at me.

Redbird, redbird, what do you see?
I see a yellow duck looking at me.

With the book in hand, most five-year-olds can "read" this selection during the earliest formal reading lessons. This is not to say that they would have mastered all of the words in isolation, or even all of the letter sounds. But in the student's mind, he is *reading* a real book, and that is exciting! All of the other elements of reading will come in time, with lots of practice and good instruction.

Predictable books

The key to using real literature at the very beginning of formal reading instruction is in using books that are predictable. In an article by Lynn K. Rhodes (1981) titled "I can read! Predictable books as resources for reading and writing instruction," she discusses the characteristics of predictable books. They are as follows:

◆ **Predictable books have a repetitive pattern.** Children can quickly follow and read along with the book after the first few pages.

◆ **They are about concepts that are very familiar to most early readers.** The children can easily identify with the story line and the characters.

◆ **There is a good match between the text and its illustrations.** This is an important key in a book's readability. In the selection from *Brown Bear, Brown Bear* above, the pictures that accompany the text essentially tell the story for the child after he has become familiar with the pattern.

◆ **Many predictable books use elements of rhyme and rhythm to increase the overall predictability of the book.** Once the child catches the rhythm or the rhyming pattern, it enhances his ability to predict what will come next.

◆ **Many also use a cumulative pattern as the story progresses.** A familiar example of a story that has a cumulative pattern is *The Gingerbread Man* where each of the fugitive cookie's pursuers is added to the narrative as the story reaches the climax.

◆ **Stories that are familiar to a child also enhance their predictability.** It is easy for most children to predict what the wolf will say in *The Three Little Pigs* because of their prior experiences with the story.

◆ **Familiar sequences are often characteristic of predictable books.** Eric Carle, in his book *The Very Hungry Caterpillar*, uses two sequences that are familiar to most young children—numbers and the days of the week:

On Monday he ate through one apple.
But he was still hungry.

On Tuesday he ate through two pears,
but he was still hungry.

Why use predictable books?

The primary reason for using these books in the earliest instructional sessions has to do with motivation. In traditional phonics-based programs, the child has to wait until he has mastered some basic elements of reading before he is able to venture into the world of "real" books. Because of this delay, he may become confused about the purposes or value of reading. The rewards of learning to read may be perceived as being so far off into the future that the child gives up hope. It is not unlike having to wait until one is sixteen years old before being allowed to drive. With most six-year-olds, delayed gratification equals no gratification!

Classifying a child as either a reader or a nonreader does not reflect the latest thinking on literacy development.

This may be a good time to digress and discuss the issue of reading readiness, or the belief that there comes a point in each child's life when he is ready to become a reader. Classifying a child as either a reader or a nonreader does not reflect the latest thinking on literacy development. Recall the earlier discussions in Chapters 2 and 3 about language acquisition and early readers. Given this information, it is more appropriate to consider the literacy development of children as being on a continuum of increasing competence. To categorize a child as either a reader or a nonreader is misleading, and it implies that he is somehow deficient until someone comes along and tells him how to read. It does not take into account the God-given ability to learn language, both spoken and written, that he has been demonstrating since his birth. Marie Clay (1966) coined the term *emergent literacy* to describe this process of a child becoming increasingly literate. In becoming a fluent reader, a person goes through many stages that are similar to a child who is learning a spoken language. Even a baby who has learned to control the intensity of his crying or cooing has demonstrated his control over certain elements of speech. We would be mistaken to classify him as a "noncommunicator" because he is not speaking the language fluently.

Predictable books provide a means for an emergent reader to practice the many behaviors that make up the act of reading.

Predictable books provide a means for an emergent reader to practice the many behaviors that make up the act of reading. Concepts about the printed word and book handling skills are learned through experience during read-aloud times and during the child's initial experiences with predictable books. Some of these concepts and skills include:

◆ the idea that print contains an exact message

◆ the difference between letters and words

- ◆ some individual letter sounds and words

- ◆ the one-to-one correspondence between spoken and printed words

- ◆ the left-to-right progression of print

- ◆ the top-to-bottom progression of lines on a page

- ◆ the return sweep at the end of each line

- ◆ the front and back of a book

- ◆ the page-by-page progression of a book

- ◆ expressive and fluent reading

- ◆ the practice of correcting oneself when mistakes (miscues) occur, to maintain meaning

Perhaps you have never considered the importance of these conventions in reading or what is the best, most effective way to teach them. An emergent reader who has participated in many read-aloud sessions has learned most of these conventions by the time he begins practicing them on his own as he reads predictable books. Rarely does the adult/teacher need to provide direct instruction on any of these concepts. Concepts about print and book handling skills are more thoroughly and efficiently learned through experience and practice.

Stanovich has indicated that the sheer amount of print that is processed by a person has a positive effect on his reading vocabulary/word recognition skills and on his knowledge in general (1994). This is true no matter how skilled the reader is or how low his ability. Using predictable books provides the best way for a child to be exposed to much print even though the child has had little formal instruction or experience. These books use many of the high-frequency words that are so important in our language. Many opportunities to overlearn these words will arise, thereby helping the child to become a fluent reader.

Reading is not just sounding out letters one after another, it is not simply saying one word after another, nor is it being perfectly accurate—it is making sense of print.

Using predictable books in the initial stages of a formal reading program allows the emergent reader to utilize everything he has learned about reading up to that point. They are like a lightning rod where all knowledge about reading processes can be discharged. The enthusiasm that is released in the child as a result of this discharge will provide valuable energy as the texts become more difficult, and the instruction grows more focused and intense.

My soapbox . . .

Reading is comprehension. We read for one reason—to get the author's message. Reading is not just sounding out letters one after another, it is not simply saying one word after another, nor is it being perfectly accurate—it is making sense of print. This should be the first and primary idea taught, demonstrated, and established in the child's formal reading program. A good read-aloud background will have already laid this foundation in the child's experience. Using predictable books will build upon that foundation.

"Prediction is the core of reading." Frank Smith, the author of *Understanding Reading* (1988), repeatedly drives this idea home. Prediction and comprehension are intricately tied together. Smith goes on to explain, "Prediction means asking questions, and comprehension means being able to get some of the questions answered." Effective readers engage in a wide range of prediction strategies while they read. These strategies span the range from thinking about style ("Knowing this author, he will probably introduce some bizarre element next"), to predicting events in a story ("I bet the butler did it"), to confirming expected word or phonic elements ("The Pony Express rider jumped on his h_____"). Their prior experiences with stories, print, and life in general are what enable readers to process the text so efficiently in this manner.

A good reading teacher can help students learn prediction skills, but once again, these skills are better learned through interaction with stories—lots of them. Reading predictable books helps a young reader to flow fluently through text because his expectations about what comes next are repeatedly confirmed. It's just good practice, and practice makes perfect!

A bibliography of predictable books for young readers

In Appendix A at the back of this book I've included a bibliography of books that you can use. The books are divided into levels of increasing difficulty. At the beginning of each level is a description of the features of the books on that level. You can add your own favorites by comparing yours to books with similar features.

Theory into practice

I've discussed the theory related to using predictable books in the early stages of a reading program. By now, you are probably wondering how an effective program should progress. With all this theory in mind, we are now ready to begin looking at the specific methods you should use as you move into a more formal reading program with your child.

CHAPTER 6:
Preparing for Formal Lessons

One point of clarification . . .

In this chapter you will notice that I am writing primarily to parents who are teaching their own children to read at home. This is the ideal situation, since a parent has more control over the child's home environment than anyone else. Adults tutoring children who are not their own can still incorporate many of the suggestions contained in this chapter to establish a foundation for formal literacy instruction. If the child has not been immersed in reading and writing at home, do what you can to add these kinds of experiences to the child's background!

Moving into formal instruction

I am going to assume that all the elements of a literate environment have been in place in your home. First of all, you have encouraged the growth of your child's oral language skills by surrounding her with sounds, songs, rhymes, and conversation. From her earliest days in the cradle you talked to her, sang to her, and read to her. You are responsive to her attempts to communicate. You shape her knowledge of the conventions of oral language by gently and positively correcting her attempts to learn its complexities.

You are a good role model for your child. She sees you reading for pleasure and information regularly. You have been reading aloud to her frequently, and your read-aloud sessions together have been times when she was free, even encouraged, to ask lots of questions about the story and the conventions of print. Possibly your child has attempted to read whole stories or parts of familiar stories to you. You have looked at the pictures in the book together and discussed how they relate to the text and whether they match with the images you make in your head. You have used your finger to follow the words at times, and you've talked about the left-to-right, top-to-bottom direction we follow when we read words. Maybe you have even looked at individual words or letters, and talked about the differences between the two.

At other times you have worked with your child in learning her ABC's. Possibly she is an avid fan of *Sesame Street* or some other preschool television program. You have played letter games with her on the computer or while driving in the car. She has helped you write the weekly shopping list or notes to family members. She can "read" some words in her environment like *McDonald's* or *Cheerios*. She can write her name and maybe a few other names or words. In short, you have created an atmosphere where the written word is presented to her in a multitude of ways that are meaningful and enjoyable.

In short, you have created an atmosphere where the written word is presented to her in a multitude of ways that are meaningful and enjoyable.

If these elements have been missing in your home to this point, it is not too late to start! Your child will benefit from these kinds of daily experiences prior to introducing a formal literacy program. They will lay the foundation that will make your more explicit instruction in reading and writing the next logical and natural step to take.

If these elements have been a regular part of your routine since your child was a baby, then she may suddenly blossom in her ability to unlock the secrets of print with no formal program of instruction. If not, don't panic! By follow-ing the guidelines in the next few chapters and by being purposeful in your instruction, your child will learn to read, and you both will have fun in the process!

I see no reason to begin formal lessons until the child is approximately five or six. But if your child is younger than this and is a real go-getter, and the informal program de-scribed above seems like it's just not enough, go right ahead and start. You'll know when you are going too fast. Just remember that reading always needs to be enjoyable and meaningful. If your child gets irritable or bored as you spend time with books, ask yourself a few ques-tions. Am I pushing too hard? Would it hurt to back off and just spend a few more weeks or months in an informal read-aloud program? Am I letting my child lead by allowing her to pick out books or activities? Am I acting as though we are under some kind of mastery dead-line? Do I get angry when she is struggling with a concept or ability? If you are still not sure what is wrong, ask the child what would make things better. Try to adjust so that you are both enjoying the process.

> *Just remember that reading always needs to be enjoyable and meaningful.*

Use the "Foundational Concepts about Books and Print" checklist at the end of this chapter as an informal guide to early literacy behaviors that your child might be demonstrating. Build awareness of these behaviors and conventions into your sessions together. It is not necessary that she be fluent in each before starting a formal program, but they should be the most basic elements established in the early sessions. Come back to this checklist regularly and check off items as they become part of your child's repertoire. She will pick up most of these behaviors along the way as you read with her, so you do not need to make them the topics of specific lessons. You might just casually mention what you are doing, like "Do you notice how I'm reading across the page like this?" or "Have you ever wondered what this little dot means?" Of course, if the child asks about specific behaviors, express delight that she is curious as you give her answers.

Learning about letters and their sounds

As I've mentioned before, your child will probably pick up most of the letter names naturally as you go about a literate family life. But there are some particular things you can do to increase his awareness of letters and their associated sounds. Once again, I am not necessarily recommending a letter-learning program. These are some things you can do prior to and during the early stages of formal reading lessons to increase letter awareness.

◆ Begin with her name or some other very important word. Teach her how to make the letters in the word, saying them as you write. Use very explicit verbal instructions as you make each letter. For example, to make an upper case *A*, you would say "Start at the top and draw a line down this way. Then start in the same place at the top and draw another line down this way. Then make a line going across that touches the two. This is an upper case A!" By the way, it is usually preferable to use the terms "upper case" and "lower case" to avoid confusion. Using the words "big" and "little" may confuse the child if she thinks you are talking about the physical size of the letter instead of its case. You may develop a shorter code in your verbal descriptions as you work with letters. For example, in making a lower case *m*, I've found the directions "down, hump, hump" to be very effective.

◆ Add other names or important words to his repertoire of known words in the same way.

◆ Keep an alphabet book made from blank typing paper or some other blank paper. Avoid using lined paper at this point. It is hard enough for a child to learn the formation of the letters without forcing him to fit them into a specified space. In fact, making the letters bigger at first may make them easier to learn. Each page in the book is for the next letter, with a perfect upper and lower case sample letter drawn by you at the top of each page. There is no reason why you shouldn't put the pages in alphabetical order, but you do not have to teach the letters in this order. If your child's name is Mary, the letter *M* in its upper and lower case forms may be the first letter learned; if John, *J* might be the first letter. Draw or glue in pictures of things that start with the letter and label them. It is helpful to use words/pictures that begin with the standard sound.

You would not want to use the word *sugar* on the *S* page, for example, because the child may confuse the /sh/ with the /s/ sound. Add to the pages as you encounter new words or letters. Review the pages frequently, and keep the book handy as you read books together.

◆ As your child learns new letters, you may want to develop a specific list of anchor words (one word for each letter) that begins with the standard sound of the letter. These words can be used as reference words by you as you instruct the child. The anchor word for each letter should be written on that letter's page in the alphabet book. A perfect anchor word for the /s/ sound would be *snake* because a snake embodies the shape of the word. Mary might best remember /m/ because of her name, but Billy might remember *McDonald's* better—the "golden arches" resemble a large *m* in his mind. Since the vowels are particularly tricky, I'd like to recommend the following anchor words for them:

> **a - apple**
> **e - egg**
> **i - igloo**
> **o - octopus**
> **u - umbrella**

The initial sound of each of the above words represents its most common short form. But refrain from using the terms *long* or *short* with your child for now.

These word connections can be very powerful for children who have a hard time remembering. I recall working with a six-year-old boy named Jacob. We were reading together in a book titled *Our Family*. It has repeating text on each page that says "We like going to the ____," with a picture of the place above the sentence; places like the park, the beach, mini-golf, etc. He was reading the book primarily from memory, but I was having him point at the words and watching first letters as he read. How Jacob responded to the book was really cute and somewhat instructive. He kept stumbling over the word *we*, wanting instead to say "Us like going to the beach." I stopped him and said "Jacob, let's look at this first word. You said 'Us like going . . .' This word starts with *W*. What sound does *W* have?" He looked at me and started to explore different sounds, hoping that he'd stumble upon the right one. I said "*W* sounds like /w/." Immediately he started singing *The Lion Sleeps Tonight*.

He had heard it in the movie *The Lion King*. The part that helped him was where it goes "*A-we-ma-wep-a-we-ma-wep* . . ." The letter *w* reminded him of the sounds from that song. It was really perfect that the word was *we* because it sounds just like the beginning of that phrase.

The next day I handed him the book and read the title. He started right off reading "Us like going to the b . . ." then he stopped. He looked at me with puzzlement on his face. I said nothing and I didn't have to. On his own, he went back

> *These word connections can be very powerful for children who have a hard time remembering.*

to the beginning of the line, pointed at *We*, and began to sing his phrase very quietly. Then he read "We like going to the beach." On the next page he started to read "Us like . . ." Then he stopped, sang, and corrected himself again. I was so excited, and I had to keep myself from laughing. But when he was through, I congratulated him enthusiastically for noticing that the word and what he was saying didn't match, and for correcting himself.

Whenever possible, help your child to make connections between all aspects of what she is learning.

This story illustrates a very important point that you will want to remember. Whenever possible, help your child to make connections between all aspects of what she is learning. If you had just learned the letter *T* together, look for ways to draw her attention to the letter when it comes up in reading aloud, writing a note to Dad, or on *Sesame Street*. These connections are very powerful, and they will help your child to understand the continuity of spoken and written language. They will also help her to remember the details of language much as Jacob did in the example above.

- ◆ You may want to start a journal with your child. Making regular entries provides meaningful practice in letter formation, sounds, and helps to develop the foundational awareness that print conveys an exact message.

- ◆ Some people have found it helpful to make labels for items around the house, using post-it notes or index cards and tape. This teaches letter and word awareness. Once again, it is important that you write the letters carefully in the form that you want your child to learn.

◆ Letter toys and games provide another avenue for letter learning. Magnetic letters are an important tool that you will be using regularly in formal lessons, so go ahead and purchase a set of upper and lower case letters and put them on the refrigerator where your child can have access to them. Other board and computer games that provide letter practice are also helpful and enjoyable.

◆ Use other media to practice writing the letters. Dry erase boards, magic slates, Magna Doodles, chalkboards, watercolor paints, and sand in cookie sheets provide variety. They add other sensory data to the child's experience with letters.

Letter checklists

At the end of this chapter is a letter identification checklist that you can use to monitor your child's progress. Keep track of whether the child can identify the letter's name (for both upper and lower case), its most common sound, and a word that starts with the letter. Update the chart as new letters are learned.

Also at the end of this chapter is a letter-identification check sheet to use with your child. All upper and lower case letters are on the sheet—out of order so that the child won't be able to sing the alphabet! You will notice that the other forms of *a* and *g* are also on the list: **a** and **g**. These are called "Printer's A" and "Printer's G," and you will find them more often than the ball and stick forms in printed material. The student simply needs to identify them as a different form of the letters. This sheet is not to be used as a handwriting model for the child. It is simply an assessment tool for you to use if you wish.

Letter reversals

Children will reverse letters as they are learning them. In my experience teaching second grade, at least half of the children frequently reversed *b, d, p,* and *q* at the beginning of the school year. It is not unusual, so don't panic or call the Dyslexia Society for advice! You simply need to find ways to help the child remember—ways that work for her. For example, I have tried several successful strategies in helping children with *b* and *d* reversals:

◆ Show the child that a lower case *b* is "hiding" inside the upper case *B*. Draw a lower case *b* then make it into an upper case *B* by adding the top part.

◆ The word *bed* is fairly easy to remember because of its shape—it looks like a bed. The *b* comes first just like when we say the alphabet.

◆ If the child holds her hands in front of her, with the palms inward, then points up with her index fingers, at the same time curling under her other fingers and thumb, her left hand is in the general shape of a lower case *b* and her right hand is in the shape of a lower case *d*. Once again, from left to right they are in alphabetical order.

With a little imagination, you can invent creative ways to help your child when she struggles with basic memory items.

Remember what I've said about not digressing into a formalized letter-learning program devoid of any real, contextual experience with print. Isolated letter work should occur sporadically within the context of sharing books and writing for real purposes. In this way, the child will not lose sight of why we learn our letters. It is not an end in itself; rather, it enables her to join what some writers have called "the literacy club" (Smith, 1986). The literacy club, just like the spoken language club, is open to everyone. Children are welcomed into these clubs by fluent language users who help to open the way for less experienced members. By our continued public enjoyment of written language, we make the prospect of gaining membership into the literacy club exciting and something worth seeking. Of course, just one venture into the world of print qualifies a child to join!

Isolated letter work should occur sporadically within the context of sharing books and writing for real purposes.

A lesson format—as you think about beginning formal lessons

I'm going to suggest a basic format for you to follow as you move toward formal lessons.* A lesson should last somewhere between 30 and 45 minutes, generally speaking. You will need at least 30 minutes for the child to adequately acquire each lesson component.

The major difference between formal lessons and what you have been doing informally up to this point is this—the child will now be expected to do most of the reading work.

The major difference between formal lessons and what you have been doing informally up to this point is this—the child will now be expected to do most of the reading work. You will certainly be doing some modeling, directing, and teaching, but if you want the child to become a fluent, strategic reader, you will need to let him work through problems while you wait, giving only minimal help when necessary to keep him going. It will be a hard change for you, but it is very rewarding when a child works things out on his own.

You may remember reading groups when you were in school. Often the teacher directed the children to take turns

*Many of the ideas presented in the following pages are patterned after the lesson format suggested by Marie Clay (1985, 1993b).

reading the story out loud—round-robin reading is the term for this practice. Think about what would happen when the current reader hesitated for more than one second. The difficult word was shouted out by several children or by the teacher before the reader could have enough time to figure it out on his own. Most struggling readers learn that if they wait long enough, others will supply them with the word. DO NOT let this happen in your lessons! DO NOT let your child become dependent on you when he gets stuck. Instead wait . . . then wait . . . then wait a little more while the child calls up everything you've taught him to that point. If he simply can't get the word, then prompt him with a cue that he could have easily tried on his own if he had remembered. If that doesn't help, then try another easily accessible cue. But more on that later! Just remember who needs to be doing most of the work!

Here is a general order of activities for a typical lesson:

1. **Begin by rereading several familiar books or part of a longer book** for fluency practice and general strategy instruction.

2. **Do a reading of the current "new" book**, one that is on the cutting edge of the child's abilities.

3. **Work on letter identification, word families, or other letter/sound activities.**

4. **Write a short story together**, usually only one or two sentences long. This gives the child practice in hearing sounds in words and recording them.

5. If the child is ready, **introduce a new book** and read it once or twice.

That's it! One key principle to remember is that in every activity where reading or writing is broken down into its component parts, you will do so *after* the child has experienced the whole first. This is one major difference between this reading program and the packaged phonics programs frequently used by parents at home. There is an obvious purpose behind the letter work that is being done—it is so we can better read the books we enjoy together.

For a week or so prior to beginning lessons, check out from the local library some of the predictable books listed in the appendix. As you read them with your child, determine her relative skill level. Get a feel for what kinds of books are easy for her to read on her own and what books are more challenging. The simplest books in the Emergent and Preprimer 1 levels will be easy for most children to "read" because of the pictures and/or repetitive text. Introduce a new book a day as you practice reading the more familiar books for fluency. Help her to be expressive when she reads, and encourage her to follow the words with her finger as you model how to do it.

> *One key principle to remember is that in every activity where reading or writing is broken down into its component parts, you will do so after the child has experienced the whole first.*

You will also want to be gathering together some teaching materials and the things you will need for your records. The amount of detail that you keep in your records is up to you and your state's legal requirements, if you are home schooling. I recommend keeping track of the child's foundational concept development and letter identification knowledge, using the forms at the end of this chapter. I also recommend using and keeping a daily lesson plan sheet. It can also double as a journal of sorts since you will record both your plans and what you actually do on the same sheet (also at the end). The child's records may be kept in a large three-ring binder. Many teachers work out of a manila folder through the week and then transfer lesson plans into the binder at the end of the week. You may also want to keep a list of books read in the folder as well as an alphabetized list of known words. See these forms at the end of this chapter.

You will want to have a simple book made from blank copy or typing paper for the child's daily story writing.

You will want to have a simple book made from blank copy or typing paper for the child's daily story writing. What works well is to go to your local copy service and have them bind 100 or so pages together with a plastic spine on the long side of the paper. You can do the same thing at home by punching your own holes and using chrome rings to bind the paper. I like to go the plastic spine route because the book made in this way is more durable, and it opens up perfectly flat. This is important, since the child will be writing in the book.

Some other things you will need are thin watercolor markers or writing crayons, pencils, and some white *Post-it* correction tape—three-quarters to one inch wide. This is used to correct (cover up) the child's errors when writing. You will need a box or basket for these things, and you will need a larger, rectangular plastic basket or durable cardboard box for storing the books the child is currently reading. I've already mentioned that you will be using a dry erase board, or a small chalkboard, or some other type of alternate writing surface, and a cookie tray with a set of upper and lower case magnetic letters.

All of this may seem like a lot, but you probably have many of these items at home. They are tools that will have very practical uses as you work with your child. Just remember, you could be spending much more money on a sequenced phonics package that is far more complicated than the program we will learn!

In the next chapters, we will learn about processes and strategies to use in working with your child as you read books and write stories together. I will tell you where in the lesson each strategy can be utilized, and how to follow your child's lead during the times you work together. You will soon become a natural at using these strategies, and your child will become a strategic reader in the process!

Record-keeping forms

On the following pages are some forms that you can freely copy for use in your program. Set your copier to enlarge these forms so they will be easier to use.

Basic Concepts about Books and Print

(Generally in order of increasing complexity)

Child's Name _____

- ❏ Can identify the front and back cover of a book
- ❏ Knows that books have titles
- ❏ Knows that the print on the page conveys the message
- ❏ Knows that the print conveys an exact message
- ❏ Understands that the pictures on a page match with the story/words on that page
- ❏ Knows where to start reading on the page
- ❏ Knows that we read from left to right in individual words and across the line
- ❏ Can make a return sweep down and to the left to start next line
- ❏ Knows about page to page progression as we read, left page before right
- ❏ Knows the difference between a single word and a single letter
- ❏ Can point at one word at a time as you read slowly (one-to-one match)
- ❏ Knows what is meant by the terms first/beginning and last/end
- ❏ Can identify at least some letters by name and/or sound
- ❏ Is beginning to understand the difference between lower and upper case letters
- ❏ May notice basic punctuation marks—has possibly inquired about them

Letter Identification Checklist

Child's Name _____

Letter	Upper	Lower	Sound	Word	Letter	Upper	Lower	Sound	Word
A, a					N, n				
B, b					O, o				
C, c					P, p				
D, d					Q, q				
E, e					R, r				
F, f					S, s				
G, g					T, t				
H, h					U, u				
I, i					V, v				
J, j					W, w				
K, k					X, x				
L, l					Y, y				
M, m					Z, z				

Letter Identification Check Sheet

Child's Name _____

a	d	g	j	m	p
s	v	y	b	e	h
k	n	q	t	w	z
c	f	i	l	o	r
u	x	**a**	**g**	A	D
G	J	M	P	S	V
Y	B	E	H	K	N
Q	T	W	Z	C	F
I	L	O	R	U	X

Lesson Plan/Journal

Child's Name _____ Date _____

Activity	Observations/Teaching Points
Familiar Books Rereading Titles:	
New Book Reading (introduced at end of last lesson) Title:	
Letter/Word Work Letter(s) or Word(s):	
Story writing Sentence:	
New Book Introduction Title: Introduction:	

Books Read

Child's Name _____

Date	Title	Level
____	_____	____
____	_____	____
____	_____	____
____	_____	____
____	_____	____
____	_____	____
____	_____	____
____	_____	____
____	_____	____
____	_____	____
____	_____	____
____	_____	____
____	_____	____
____	_____	____
____	_____	____

Known Words

Child's Name _____

A	B	C
D	E	F
G	H	I
J	K	L
M	N	O
P	Q	R
S	T	U
V	W	X
Y	Z	endings,families,chunks

CHAPTER 7:
Book Reading and Strategy Development

Real books, real strategies

What makes this program different from other at-home reading programs is the use of children's literature as the medium for instruction. The bulk of teaching will occur as you and the child are engaged in reading real stories—books not written with instructional ends in mind. When stories are written using only "easy" words or to teach specific phonic elements, they end up sounding artificial. Reflect back to "Sam's ham and Dan's ax" in Chapter 5 or to your own days of "Look, Dick, look. See Spot run. Run, Spot, run!" Not very rich or engaging!

The parts of the lesson that have to do with text are the familiar readings at the beginning, reading the previous day's new book, and the introduction of another new book at the end of the lesson. The child will also be reading stories that he has written during the writing segment. Text readings have a dual purpose:

♦ to give the child a chance to put together everything he knows about reading on more familiar texts, and

♦ to give him a chance to use the strategies he is learning on unfamiliar text.

These readings also provide opportunities for instruction, not only in strategic reading, but also to practice letter/sound correspondence (phonics). In this chapter, we will not be focusing on phonics instruction as a separate entity, but on how knowledge of letters and language helps us to find the message in the print.

What are strategies?

I prefer to use the word *strategies* rather than *skills* in order to break away from the notion of a predetermined sequence of increasingly difficult bits of knowledge. This has been the common definition of *skills* in the past. I hope that in the earlier chapters I have effectively explained why this notion is unacceptable. Children are incredible problem solvers when it comes to learning language. Armed with an effective set of strategies, they will use these problem-solving abilities in reading and comprehending new text. Your job as the teacher is to help the child shape these language-learning strategies, which are variations of the ones he used in learning oral language.

When reading, we use a variety of cues to extract the message from the print. Letter decoding is only one cue that we use. It is obviously an effective tool, but it is not the only one available. This illustration will help to define the sources of the cues we use when we read (Burke, 1972).

PRINT

GRAMMAR

MEANING

Meaning is the core of the reading process. The reason that we read is to get the meaning from (or to make sense of) the text. The constant "movie" that is being played out mentally as one reads is one source for meaning cues. While he is reading, the beginning reader is working to make new information fit in with what is already there. Pictures on the page are another source of meaning cues. In easy, predictable books, these pictures provide a very rich and supportive set of meaning cues. As the difficulty level of the books increases, the picture cues become less supportive and the burden is shifted more to the child's making sense of the text himself. Throughout your instruction, you need to emphasize that getting the meaning of the text is the primary goal of reading. Encourage the child to keep building a meaningful story in his head as he reads.

The rules of grammar that we use in speaking are carried over to the printed word. We have idioms and turns of phrase that a child learns when he starts to talk. Writers write in ways that fit the rules we use when we communicate. These rules are not broken in a printed story. So if the child reads a sentence that does not sound grammatically correct, he may realize that an error was made in reading the text.

Throughout your instruction, you need to emphasize that getting the meaning of the text is the primary goal of reading. Encourage the child to keep building a meaningful story in his head as he reads.

Finally, symbols in the form of print on a page are the vehicles for carrying the meaning to the reader. Once again, these symbols are placed on the page in conventional ways. We read from left to right, top to bottom, and words are spelled in ways that have been agreed upon over time. If our written language was a perfect one-to-one match between specific sounds and specific letters, it would be much easier to learn to read. But the old adage "Rules are made to be broken" is especially true in our written language. Because of the inconsistencies in printed English, learning to read is a tricky thing indeed.

Notice in the diagram on page 93 that the three language systems appear to blend into each other. This is to show that the systems are not separate entities. We use all three systems simultaneously and efficiently to extract meaning from print. Consider the following incomplete sentence:

The cowboy jumped on the h____ and rode out of town.

Most children could easily supply the missing word, or at least one that made total sense, even though only one letter is there. This is because we expect stories to make sense—to have meaning. Most children would fill in the word *horse* because of their knowledge of cowboys and what they ride, and because of the *h* cue at the beginning. It would not work to fill in the word *have* because it does not make sense, and because our set of grammatical rules does not permit the word *have* to be used after the article *the*. A child who was only looking at the print without thinking about meaning might be more likely to fill in a word that does not make sense or is not grammatically correct. Good readers use all three cueing systems in an integrated fashion to constantly monitor their reading.

When a reader makes an error while reading, it is because he misinterpreted one or more cues. You, as the child's teacher, need to help him learn how to use several cues at a time to be an effective reader. He needs to check constantly meaning cues with grammar cues and print cues to make sure it is all fitting together. In the example above, the child might fill in the word *pony* and it would make sense and be grammatically correct. But he would be ignoring the print cue that was there. Checking all three cueing sources against each other keeps this from happening.

When a child makes an error in text reading, you need to quickly analyze his error. What cue(s) did he use? What cue(s) did he ignore? What is the most effective way to alert him to his error? If you wait for a little bit, will he self-correct without any help from you? Are you beginning to see why saying "sound it out" is not always the most effective help you can give?

Book introductions

With the above discussion in mind, we need to talk about the best way to introduce a new book to the child.* As you read with her, you will quickly learn about her use of cues when she encounters new or difficult text. If she normally falls back into using letter cues only, then you will want to have her think about the meaning of the story. In early reading instruction, the pictures in the books you are using are an important source of meaning for the reader. Pictures will support her early attempts at reading the book. Research has shown that good readers create vivid images in their heads as they read. Pictures in picture books support this image creation, and they provide a source of meaning when the text is challenging.

On the other hand, if the reader has a tendency to ignore the text and key in totally to the pictures, then you

This way of introducing books was developed by Marie Clay (1985, 1993b).

will need to prompt regularly her attention to the print. This is why teaching the child to point at the words is so important in the early lessons. In the books listed in the appendix, most of the easiest books have easy-to-remember text with few variations. Teach your child to point under the words and look at them as she reads the book. If she makes an error, like saying *pony* instead of *horse*, then you can prompt her back to the text.

So when you introduce a new book, review the entire book prior to reading it. Tell the child the title and talk about each page with her. Look at the pictures together, *using the language in the book as you talk!* By doing so you will familiarize the child with the language and special words used in the story. For example, if the story uses the word *kitten*, do not confuse the child by talking about the *cat*. If the story uses a repeated line such as *They went to the store*, *They went to the park*, etc., do not say, "Where did they *go*?" Instead say, "Oh, look, they *went* to the store! Where do you think they *went* next?" But remember, you are not reading the book to the child. Try to carry on a natural conversation about the story using the words in the story.

So when you introduce a new book, review the entire book prior to reading it. Tell the child the title and talk about each page with her.

It is a good idea to have the child locate one or two important words in the story prior to the first full reading. These should be words that are somewhat new to the child. Using the example above, you may want to prompt the child to the word *went* since it is a frequently used word. During your introduction, stop on a page where *went* is used in the text. Tell the child to say *went*, then ask her what letter she would expect to see at the beginning. She should say "w." If she doesn't, then tell her that she hears a *w* at the beginning. Then have her locate *went* by scanning the text and finding a word that starts with *w*. If you have her locate *went* once or twice more throughout the introduction, then she will be ready to read the word when she attempts the story.

As the child becomes more proficient in later lessons, have her look at the new book prior to the first reading and tell you what the story is about. This develops the good habit of orienting oneself to a story or book before beginning to read.

The first reading

Now the child is ready to read the new book as independently as possible. If you have chosen an appropriately difficult book, the child should be able to read much of it on his own, but he will also encounter some problems that will challenge what he knows about reading.

Read the title with him; then have him start on the first page of text. Remember to have him use his finger as he reads, pointing crisply to each word. But do not allow him to "call" words; that is, to read . . . each . . . word . . . one . . . by . . . one . . . as if he were reading a list. This is a bad habit that you should gently discourage right from the start. If the child tries to read this way, wait until he is finished with a page, then model more fluent, expressive reading for him. The best place to encourage fluent reading is on a book that is already familiar to him, however, so don't dwell too much on it during the first readings of a new book.

Allow the child to work through difficulties with as little help from you as possible. Any help that you do offer should be done quickly and directly so that the child's comprehension of the story is not lost. Other more specific techniques to use to encourage strategy development will be discussed later in this chapter. Just remember that you are working to make the child an independent reader, and your prompts and teaching points should be examples of the kind of thinking he should do on his own. For example, suppose the child was reading and got stuck on the word *bike.* It would not help the child to say "This is one of those two-wheeled things that you ride." He would not be able to generate this thought on his own, so do not offer it to him as a prompt. Instead, suggest that he look at the picture, think about the story, look at the first letter of the word, and try again. In later lessons, you may suggest that he look at the word to find a part that he knows. He may already know the work *like,* for example, so he might be able to get *bike* by noticing the *-ike* ending. If he does what you say and is able to get the word, comment positively on how he figured that out all by himself. Tell him what he did that worked, then go on. If he did try your suggestions and he still could not get the word, then give him a more specific cue to consider. Point to the picture, tell him to think about what the person in the story

Allow the child to work through difficulties with as little help from you as possible.

is going to ride, or some other prompt. When he does get the word with your help, don't just say "Right!" Ask him how he knows that it is *bike*. He should point to the picture, the *b* in *bike*, or to some other logical cue.

When the child has finished reading the book with your support as described above and in the next section, you may want to pick out one or two specific points to emphasize as teaching points. Do not overwhelm the child with too many instructional concepts. Choose the ones that are on the cutting edge of his abilities, ones that are easily within his grasp to master.

Reading again for fluency

Because the first reading was probably interrupted several times for instruction, have the child read the book again, this time focusing on reading for fluency. You may want to help the child by modeling how a line should be read, or by reading right along with him. You can hesitate on problem words to see if he can get them on his own. Always comment on the good things that the child has done, trying to be as specific as possible so he will want to continue with helpful strategies.

Books and lessons

I need to clarify where all of this fits into the lesson. You start each lesson rereading several books that the child has read previously. You may do some quick teaching during these readings, but they are primarily for fluency practice. They help to get him warmed up, and they give him an opportunity to use familiar texts to put together everything he has learned to this point. After the familiar readings, you have the child read the most recently introduced new book, probably from the previous lesson. Since he has spent only a few minutes with this book, it is a good time for you to monitor the kind of progress he is making. Is he using the strategies you have been teaching him? Does he actively work on problems without giving up immediately? Does he self-correct frequently? Is this book too easy or hard for him? One rule of thumb: If the child is making more than one uncorrected error for each ten words in the story, then it is probably too difficult. A 90% or better accuracy rate is necessary for comprehension to occur.

One rule of thumb: If the child is making more than one uncorrected error for each ten words in the story, then it is probably too difficult. A 90% or better accuracy rate is necessary for comprehension to occur.

The next new book is introduced at the end of the lesson as described above. The optimum program is one where a new book is introduced each day. But this may not be possible for a number of reasons. In this case, you would probably want to continue practice on the most recent new book, or on another book that is causing the child some difficulty.

Obviously, books will begin to build up in the child's book basket. As newer, more difficult books are introduced, you should remove the older, easier books from the basket.

When the child has read a book enough times to have it memorized, he may quit actively looking at the print or searching for information. This is a sure sign that the book should be removed.

Choosing new books

The list in Appendix A contains books of increasing difficulty, generally speaking. Of course, a book's difficulty is a relative thing. What is difficult for one child may not be for the next. But you should find that the books contain less repetitive text, fewer picture cues, and more words as you go to higher levels.

As you choose the child's next book, try to pick one at a level where he will be challenged, but not overwhelmingly so. If a book turns out to be too difficult, just set it aside and try another, or go ahead and use it with more support from you. The book's difficulty level is not necessarily the most important factor in considering whether to use it with the child. Any book can provide opportunities for instruction depending on how you use it, so do not be bound by the list. If your library does not stock many of the books that are recommended, pick out some others that will provide appropriate challenges for your child. Use a book for what you can get out of it. But, you will probably have more productive lessons by trying to be sensitive to a book's relative level as it compares to the others in the list.

Using the lesson plan

If you choose to use the lesson plan form in Chapter 6, then you will want to record information prior to and during the lesson. Prior to the lesson, write down the title of the new book you've chosen at the end of the form under *New Book Introduction, Title.* As you preview the book, make some notes about how you will introduce it. For example, you may want to remind yourself to use the word *kitten* instead of *cat,* or to say *went* instead of *go.* You should also record what word or words you want the child to locate prior to the first reading.

Do not record the titles of the familiar books read until the actual lesson. Many teachers let the child choose one or more of the books he reads. Of course, you will need to suggest a book from time to time as well, because the child may avoid books that are more challenging. Also, under *New Book Rereading,* record the title of the new book that was introduced at the end of yesterday's lesson.

During the lesson, record your observations or teaching points on the right side of the page. Make notes about words practiced or strategies prompted or used by the child. These notes will help as you plan the next day's lesson. Do not worry if this seems a little unclear right now. Things will fall into place as you continue reading!

Strategy development in text reading

The goal of your instruction is to help the child become a strategic reader. A strategic reader can use many cues from several sources to solve the problems he encounters while reading text. He learns these strategies as you model them and through your direct instruction. They can also be learned incidentally (through indirect instruction) as described in the chapter on early readers. Most children learn to read because of a blend of direct and indirect instruction.

The most basic concepts about print will be learned early in the child's life as he participates with you in a home literacy program that includes reading aloud and writing for real purposes. It is in this context that the child will discover all of the ideas listed on the checklist, "Foundational Concepts about Books and Print" at the end of the last chapter. By the time your child is ready to begin formal lessons, he should be familiar with most of these concepts. The few that are still tricky for him will become more clear as you work together in lessons.

The following strategies and teaching suggestions are specified by Marie Clay in the Reading Recovery program (Clay, 1993). Even though she says that the meticulous and rigorous application of these techniques will be unnecessary for most children, she assumes that the children are enrolled in a regular classroom. If you are teaching your child to read at home using the ideas in this book, *you* are the child's classroom. I include a discussion of these strategies here because they are effective with all children, not just children who are having difficulties.

One-to-one matching

The child should be able to point at each word as he reads. You can encourage this by telling him to read with his finger. If he tries but his spoken words do not match one-to-one with the text because of an error, you can:

- **ask him "Did that match?" or "Did you run out of words?"**

- **tell him to go back and try again**

- **point with the child but stop your finger at the error**

Locating known or unknown words

It is helpful at times for the child to be able to locate words that she knows in text. They act as anchors when much of the text is unfamiliar. They give her a reference point that may be helpful, especially when used with one-to-one finger pointing. You can help by:

- **telling her to go back and find the known word(s).** Then encourage her to use them as she tries again.

◆ **reading the text back to her the way she read it and asking "Were you right?"** Prompt her to known words if necessary.

◆ **having the child find an unknown word by listening for the first letter or some other known cue.** This will help her to remember the word when she reads the text.

◆ **encouraging her to reread the sentence up to the difficulty and sounding the first letter of the hard word.** You may need to do this for her so she can think about the meaning of the story and what word might fit.

Self-monitoring and cross-checking

Encourage the child to depend on his own eyes and ears when reading, and not on someone else to monitor his reading. A child develops the ability to cross-check as he learns to use meaning, grammar, and print-based cues in conjunction with each other to check his reading. The one-to-one strategies and locating strategies above are helpful in self-monitoring and cross-checking. Some other ways to encourage these behaviors follow:

◆ **Refer to meaning cues.** Tell the child to think about the story and/or to look at the picture. Remind the child about a part of the story that he has already read.

◆ **Refer to grammar cues.** Ask the child "Did that sound right?" or "Do we talk that way?"

◆ **Refer to print cues.** When the child reads a word incorrectly and does not notice, first tell him what he read. Then cover the word with your finger and say "If this word was *pony* (or whatever word he read incorrectly), what would you expect to see at the beginning (or at the end, or after the *p*, etc.)? Then have him check as you uncover the word. He should notice that his substitution did not match with the print on the page.

◆ **When the child hesitates, ask him why he stopped.** Get him to verbalize his monitoring attempts. Praise him for what he notices.

◆ **Frequently ask "How did you know?" when he successfully reads difficult words.** Telling you his successful behavior will help to make it habitual. Praise all of his attempts to work out difficulties on his own.

◆ **Extend the "How did you know?" question by asking "How else did you know?"** This should prompt the child to point to a different cue besides the primary one used to identify the word. Get him to realize that the word made sense (had meaning), it sounded right (was grammatically correct), and it looked right (in print).

Self-correction

As the term implies, self-correction occurs when the child makes an error and, because he is monitoring his reading, corrects the error on his own. Self-correcting behavior is very good and should be encouraged. It shows that the child is cross-checking one cue against another. You can encourage self-correcting in the following ways:

◆ **Encourage the child when he self-corrects.** Tell him "I liked the way you . . . "

◆ **Allow plenty of processing time when the child is having difficulty.** Do not always jump right in to offer help, especially if the child is actively working on searching for cues.

◆ **When you do need to help, prompt to a cue that is different from one he is trying.** For example, if he is trying to sound out the word and is being unsuccessful, encourage him to use a meaning or grammar cue.

◆ **Encourage the child to go back to the beginning of the sentence and reread it once he has worked out a problem.** Ask him if it is right, how he knew, etc.; then praise his efforts.

◆ **As the child becomes more proficient and confident in his reading, do not be as specific in pointing out unnoticed errors.** Say, "There was a problem in this sentence. Can you find it?"

Some other strategies

Below are a few strategies that many readers may find effective. You can introduce your child to these ideas to see if he adds them to his repertoire.

◆ **Skip over the difficult part and read on to see if some later information may help.** Then encourage him to go back to the hard part to figure it out.

◆ **Go back and review some information earlier in the book that may prove to be helpful.**

◆ **Look for familiar parts in a difficult word.** A child may recognize the word *cat* in *catch*, or he may be able to identify an ending such as *-ed* or *-ing*.

Of course, there is a whole set of strategies to use that involve the letters and sounds in the words. I have purposely discussed other, sometimes more efficient, strategies to try prior to "sounding out" a word. Remember that proficient readers use meaning and grammar-based cues in addition to cues in print, and that the use of these cues can be taught using the methods described above.

With this understanding, let's turn to the teaching of words and their parts.

CHAPTER 8:
Learning about Letters, Sounds, and Words

Awareness of print

To begin this discussion of teaching about print, it may be helpful to examine the following diagram that graphically depicts the knowledge the child should be building about the printed word in text. A child's awareness of print is usually gained in a progression shown on the chart, starting at the bottom of the pyramid.

Higher Concepts about Print

◆ using middle parts of words

◆ using ending parts of words

◆ using beginning parts of words

◆ using word shape/length

◆ locating/using known words

◆ one-to-one matching

◆ directionality (left to right, top to bottom)

◆ awareness that print carries a message

Basic Knowledge about Print

You need to be aware of what knowledge and abilities the child has when working with print, so you can always be working on her "cutting edge." For example, if she knows that the print carries the message, and she demonstrates knowledge of directionality, and she can accurately point at one word at a time as she reads, or as you read, then you know that the next ability you need to develop with her is using known words while she is reading (this will be described in the next section). Concentrate on this as you work together until the behavior is firmly established. Expecting her to function two or three levels above her current abilities will only produce frustration for you both. You may mention other concepts as you work together, but don't expect her to grasp them until she understands the earlier concepts. Pointing out that the first letter of a word didn't match with what she said is fine to bring to her attention when it occurs, but she probably won't instantly understand or incorporate this knowledge routinely in her reading until the earlier behaviors have been established.

Establishing a list of known words

As the child is experiencing the printed word in books and writing activities, she will become familiar with a list of short, high-frequency words. It is very helpful for her to have a basic sight vocabulary under her control. Now, before you start gasping at my suggestion that a sight vocabulary should be developed, please understand that I am not advocating sight reading or the look-say approach. It is normal for children to learn whole words as they are learning to read. The most frequently used word in the English language is *the*, and its pronunciation does not fit normal phonics rules. It is a prime candidate for memorization.

There are several advantages to having a list of immediately recognized words. As I mentioned in the last chapter, they act as anchors for new readers as they are pointing at text. These are high-frequency words, so they will be encountered every day. They also can be used as reference points for the child as you begin to talk about sounds and letters. For example, I use the word *the* as a reference for the *th* blend. When *th* comes up in other words, and the child hesitates, I remind her of the word *the*. I ask "Where is your tongue when you start to say *the*? That is because it starts with *th*. Any time you see *th* in a word, your tongue will go between your teeth just like it does in *the*." I may even use the dry erase board or the writing pad to talk about other words with *th*.

Some other high-frequency words that are helpful to know are:

> **a, I, am, an, and, me, my, in, is, it, at, look,**
> **see, we, go, stop, on, off, up, out, like, mom,**
> **dad, love, here, to, this . . .**

This is just a suggested list. Your child may have some words that are unique to her. One child with whom I worked knew the word *oval* before just about any others! In order to help her learn some of these words, you may want to take opportunities as they come up in text reading to provide some meaningful, concentrated practice. Let's say that the child is having trouble reading the word *in*. You could stop right in the middle of the reading, grab the magnetic letters, and make the word (on a vertical surface like the refrigerator or a file cabinet, or just on the table top since it is to be quick). Have her read it running her finger under the word from left to right as she reads. Then jumble up the letters and tell her to make the word *in*. Be sure to have her read the word again. You could have her practice writing the word on a chalkboard, dry erase board, or writing pad, reading it each time that she makes it. Some teachers provide other means of practice, such as using a wet paint brush on the chalkboard, using various color markers or crayons, using a Magna Doodle, or writing the word in a shallow cake pan half filled with sand. Whatever you do, do it quickly and get right back to the text-reading where she can use the word. When the child can write the word whenever you ask, and when she can quickly recognize it in text, then she has learned the word. Record it on her "Known Words" chart found at the end of Chapter 6. This magnetic letter work and the subsequent writing practice described above can also take place during the *Letter/Word Work* portion of the lesson. Prior to the lesson, choose a word that she has encountered in text to practice during this time.

The key to how well a child can learn new things is whether she can connect new learning to what she already knows. As you work with her, look for ways to help her make these connections. She will come across known words as she reads and writes. She will also use what she knows about letters and sounds to build new words.

Word building: A strategic way to teach phonics

The "Great Debate" has prompted much recent research into effective ways to teach letter-sound relationships. Before I talk about the recommendations that come from this research, let me review what the experts are *not* recommending. No one is recommending phonics programs where phonic generalizations are taught in isolation using "skill and drill" workbooks, flash cards, or rote memorization activities. As discussed before, the problem with these techniques is that they are separated from any meaningful literacy activities as an integral part of the program. It is important that, as the child learns about letter-sound relationships, he uses this knowledge for real literary purposes.

The term *word building* has been used to describe a phonics approach that uses the common, natural methods that novice readers use to decode words (Gunning, 1995). Young children have a natural tendency to seek out pronounceable word parts as they attempt new words. They are looking for what they know in unknown words to see if this will help them to read them. What they know may amount to single letters or to combinations of letters. They may recognize combinations that are made up of smaller known words, *f* + *in* = *fin*, or from known word parts, *s* + *ing* = *sing*. Whatever the case, an effective word-building program uses this natural tendency to help children learn decoding strategies.

Linguists, or people who study language, have given names to these word parts. In single-syllable words, the consonant or consonants at the beginning of the word are called the *onset* and the second part is called the *rime* (the part that rhymes with other words). The easiest part for children to recognize is the rime. Therefore, the easiest way to build words is to add different onsets to the same rime. (For example: n**ot**, p**ot**, h**ot**, d**ot**.)

Using word building in your reading program

Although these strategies could be used at any time during the lesson, the part of the lesson called *Letter/Word Work* is set aside for teaching letter recognition and word building. When the child knows most of her letters, and when she has established a growing list of known words, you may shift your instructional emphasis during this time to word building. I recommend planning for a particular pattern ahead of time. For example, based on the child's previous lesson, you observe that she is having trouble with the word *took*. You turn to her "Known Words" chart and discover that she already knows *look*. You decide to use her knowledge of *look* to teach other words that end with the same *-ook* rime. So you write on the lesson plan that you will make some analogies beginning with *look* and proceeding to *book, hook,* and *took.* You might even try *shook* because you know that she is familiar with the *sh* blend. You could record this on your lesson plan like this:

look
book
hook
took
shook ?

Before proceeding with an explanation of how to work with your child, let's establish some terminology. I don't recommend using the terms *onset* or *rime* with your child. They could become confusing. Instead, Marie Clay in the Reading Recovery program has simply called them *chunks*. They are parts, or chunks, of words. So you would refer to *ook* as "the *ook* chunk." Sometimes you might pronounce it as a single unit, or you might spell it out, "the o-o-k chunk." I see no problem in calling the exercise "word building." Some teachers have also referred to it as making "word families." You may not even need to give the exercise a name in working with the child. Just proceed with the activity. Here are the steps. You can use magnetic letters or writing:

1. **Make a connection**—Say "You know this word. It is *look*. Read it." (child reads *look* by running her finger under it from left-to-right as she reads) "If I put a *c* where the *l* was, that makes *cook*. You read it. Now, what would this word be?" (replace the *c* with a *b*.) If the child struggles, help her. After showing her several words, allow her to practice the new knowledge by reviewing the words with her. You can move the first letters while she reads the words, or she may want to move the letters. To start with a word the child does not know, just make or write the word, tell the child what it is, then have her make or write it herself. Then proceed with the activity.

2. **Continue building other words** by adding to the rime. Have the child read the word with her finger and make it herself as described above.

Here are some variations to the activity. They may be a little more difficult.

3. **Have the child add to the rime** by providing the necessary letters—Ask "If this is *look*, how would you make *book . . . took . . . shook?*" You may need to provide a selection of letters to choose from. The child reads each word she makes.

4. **You provide the onset, and have the child make the word by adding the rime.** Say "Here's a *t*. What would I add to make the word *took?* Here's a *b*. What would I add to make it say *book?*"

5. **Ask the child to make up other known words** using the rime, or to make up words that are new to her. Say "Do you know any other words that end like *look?* Can you try some other possibilities?" Allow the child to experiment with other letters.

6. A somewhat more difficult activity for early readers is to **provide the onset and then change the rime**. An example of this would be building from the *i* in the words *in, is,* and *it,* or from the *a* in *am, as,* and *at.* Children initially pay closer attention to the changes at the beginnings of words than at the end. Recall the print awareness pyramid at the beginning of this chapter.

7. It would logically follow, then, that the most challenging word-building activity would be **changing the middle vowel while keeping the beginning and end of the word the same.** Going from *get* to *got*, or from *sat* to *set* to *sit* are examples of this activity.

High-Frequency Rimes and Syllables

rime	example	rime	example	rime	example	rime	example	rime	example
-ab	cab	-e	me	-ice	mice	-o	no	-op	mop
-ack	tack	-ea	sea	-id	lid	-oad	toad	-ope	rope
-ad	sad	-eak	beak	-ide	ride	-oak	oak	-ot	pot
-ade	made	-eal	seal	-ie	pie	-oat	goat	-ound	round
-ag	bag	-ean	bean	-ig	pig	-ob	Bob	-out	shout
-age	page	-ear	ear	-ight	night	-ock	lock	-ow	cow
-ail	nail	-eat	eat	-ike	bike	-od	rod	-ow	crow
-ain	train	-ed	bed	-ill	hill	-og	dog	-own	clown
-ait	wait	-ee	bee	-im	him	-oice	voice	-oy	toy
-ake	cake	-eed	seed	-ime	time	-oil	boil		
-al(l)	ball	-eel	wheel	-in	pin	-oin	coin	-ub	sub
-ale	whale	-een	green	-ine	nine	-oke	joke	-uck	duck
-am	ham	-eep	jeep	-ing	ring	-old	gold	-ug	rug
-ame	name	-eet	feet	-ink	pink	-ole	mole	-um	gum
-an	pan	-ell	bell	-tion	action	-oll	roll	-un	sun
-and	sand	-en	ten	-ip	ship	-one	bone	-ture	future
-ap	map	-end	send	-ish	fish	-ong	song	-us(s)	bus
-at	cat	-ent	went	-it	hit	-ook	book	-ut	nut
-ate	gate	-et	net	-ite	kite	-ool	school		
-aw	saw			-ive	five	-oom	broom	-y	cry
-ay	hay			-ive	give	-oon	moon	-y	sunny

This list is found in an article entitled "Word Building: A Strategic Approach to the Teaching of Phonics" by Thomas G. Gunning (1995). It shows 101 of the most frequent rimes found in both single and multisyllable words. You can refer to this list to help you determine what word-building elements you can teach your child.

As you build words with the child and add new words and word chunks to the child's reading vocabulary, look for opportunities to practice what he knows. Point out familiar or recently learned words to him as you read together. He will begin to do the same. He may begin to notice familiar chunks in new words. These chunks will help him to decode the word by putting together things that he knows. If he struggles, you may need to help by covering up unfamiliar parts of words, leaving only the familiar chunk exposed. Once he reads the chunk, then uncover the whole word and help him to put it together.

As you build words with the child and add new words and word chunks to the child's reading vocabulary, look for opportunities to practice what he knows.

I've already touched on the teaching of other word chunks in the discussion of the *th* blend above. Blends (such as *bl, br, dr, fl, gr, pl, pr, st, etc.)* can best be taught by pointing them out in reading and then practicing with word-building activities. For example, the child may struggle with the word *shook.* You could check his "Known Words" chart to see if he knows any words with the *sh* blend. If he does, build from that word. The word *she* may be a known word. Using the word-building steps above, start with *she* and have him read and make the word. Then ask "What would it be if I took off the *e* and then added the -*ook* chunk?" You may need to review *look, book,* and *took.* Add *sh* to the -*ook* chunk and help him put it together. Emphasize that *sh* always sounds the same even when it comes at the end of a word. Use other known words from his list or find familiar books that use *sh* in various positions to reinforce the point. An important key in learning all of this is not only to practice word-building elements in exercises, but also to point out known words and chunks in text reading as well. Most children will begin to make connections easily on their own.

Do not let text readings be broken up by too much emphasis on individual words. Remember that the goal of reading is to get the meaning out of print.

One caution, however. Do not let text readings be broken up by too much emphasis on individual words. Remember that the goal of reading is to get the meaning out of print. Turning text reading into a word hunt party will not be ultimately beneficial to the child. Point out individual words or parts just enough to make powerful connections that will reinforce the concepts being learned.

Obviously, for these activities to be possible, the child first needs to become very familiar with a list of known words—like the ones mentioned at the beginning of the chapter. It will be somewhat frustrating for you both if you continually build from words that are unfamiliar in the first place. Once the child adds some words to his list of known words, you can start building from them. Become very familiar yourself with the words that he knows so you can seize opportunities to use them in word-building activities.

It is unnecessary to follow a prescribed sequence in what words you work with first. Remember, the beauty of this program is that you are following the *child's* lead in the quest for literacy. The most frequent phonics generalizations, such as the *long vowel-consonant-silent e* pattern (*ate, made, like, shake, etc.*) will come up repeatedly as you work with words. Just as in learning to talk, your child will begin to internalize these patterns through experience, and through talking about them as they come up in reading and writing.

Multisyllable words

As the child begins to encounter longer words in her reading, you will need to help her hear the syllables in these words. Teach her how to clap with two- and three-syllable words such as *ti / ger* or *el / e / phant*. Once she recognizes that longer words have syllables, she can try to isolate the syllables as she looks at the letters in the words. Then she can use what she knows to figure out the pronunciation of the word. Of course, in text reading, other meaning-based cues will help to identify the word as she tries to decode it.

Here are some suggestions for teaching the child to use pronounceable word parts to read longer words.

1. **Suggest that she look for parts that she knows.**
   Often, by locating and eliminating from consideration such chunks as the *-ing* or *-ed* endings, the

child can figure out the rest of the word because it contains familiar elements. The word *standing* is made up of the blend *st*, the easily familiar word *and*, and the end chunk -*ing*. Show the child that she knows all the parts of the word, and that she just needs to put them together. Compound words may thwart the child until she realizes that they are made up of two smaller words that she knows. Once the child puts everything together, she needs to check that the word makes sense in the sentence before going on (if the word was encountered in text).

2. **Present similar multisyllabic words in patterns.** Write or make the word *playing*. Clap the syllables. Decide with the child where the word should be broken. Have her read the syllables slowly and deliberately, then put it back together. Then introduce some similar words like *jumping, crying,* or *praying.* Talk about what the words have in common and how this knowledge will help in the future.

3. **Build long words from smaller, known parts.** Start with the familiar word *and.* Make the word *stand* by adding *st* to the front. Add the -*ing* chunk to the end to make *standing.* Now add the word *out* to the front making the long word *outstanding.* Of course, during each step above, the child reads the word with her finger and is engaged as much as possible in the activity. An activity like this would not be done very often. Its value is in showing the child that long words are often made from easily recognizable parts.

Your flexibility and creativity are paramount!

Remember, this is not a step-by-step program. You must look for creative ways to make helpful connections with your child. You must avoid confusing the child with examples that are not well thought out. Constantly review the strategies explained in this chapter so that you will not lock into one pattern. Be flexible but purposeful. If you have no idea why you are teaching something, chances are that the child will not have a clue as to what is going on either. And remember, these word-building strategies are not ends in themselves, nor do you use them only in the *Letter/Word Work* part of the lesson. Use them in conjunction with the text strategies explained in Chapter 7 and with the writing activities we will be talking about next. Let your lessons flow with all kinds of meaningful connections!

Recording your work

Remember to record what you do in the lesson plan. After a while, you will develop your own code to explain what you did with the child. If you quickly practice an unknown word like *in* during the familiar readings, record this on the right side of the lesson plan. Because this activity took place during the familiar readings, record your notes on the *Familiar Books Rereading* part of the plan. The *Letter/Word Work* part of the plan is where you record the activities that take place specifically during that part of the lesson. Recording activities in their contexts helps you to know later whether the word work took place during text reading or during the specific time set aside for this work. As you look over your plans each week, you may realize that you are spending too much text-reading time working on words or that you are not varying your methodology enough during the *Word Work* time.

What I've described above is how letter/sound relationships can be taught in the context of reading. Writing with the child affords another powerful opportunity to do much valuable phonics work. This is the topic of the next chapter.

CHAPTER 9:
Story Writing in
the Reading Lesson

The benefits of story writing

In this part of the lesson, the child and you will write a short story together, or you will continue a story previously started. This provides the child with practice in other aspects of reading—those having to do with hearing the sounds in words and learning to record them in print. When a child reads, he sees printed words and translates them into sounds. Reading and writing are complementary activities that help the child to become a fluent user and producer of the printed word.

The steps in writing activities are as follows:

1. **The child, with your support, generates an idea.**

2. **This idea is shaped into a story** (often just a single sentence).

3. **The story is recorded by listening to the sounds in each word.** You help the child to edit the story as you write it together.

4. **The child rereads the story.**

In early lessons, you will do much of the writing. But, as the child learns more, he will take over the work. Valuable practice in letter formation and word building will take place during this time. Even though you are working to synthesize print at the letter and word level, the ultimate focus of the activity is to produce a piece of writing that conveys a message.

A writing book or book writing?

You can vary the context in which story writing occurs in the form of the eventual product. Sometimes, you will write just to be practicing—a new sentence or very short story each day that is not connected to the previous day's work. In this case, you will want to use the bound writing pad made from copy paper that was discussed in Chapter 6. With the book turned sideways, the child writes the edited story on the bottom half. The top half is where letters and words are practiced. The rule of thumb is this: the top is strictly for practice and it can be sloppy. The finished product on the bottom half, however, should be corrected by the time the writing session is finished each day. (Clay, 1985, 1993b)

Practice

Final Copy

At other times, you may want to make a simple book with the child. Each day, you will add another page to the story until the book is completed. You can do this in one of two ways. You can work in the actual book each day, practicing in the practice book, writing the corrected story in the story book, and letting the child illustrate it after the lesson is completed. Or you may want to use the practice book to write the continuing story each day. This is like the rough draft. When the story is completed, you transfer the story to the book in final copy form and illustrate it. In either case, you will always want to have the practice book handy. It is a good place to keep the child's ever-improving work. You can refer back to it for instructional purposes, and it provides verifiable records of your work in case you should ever need to prove to someone else that valuable instruction has been going on. For these reasons, you should always date the pages in the practice book. These pages should coincide with the lesson plan for that day.

A quick note on book making—your local library will have many resources on how to make books if you want to go a notch or two above a simple book made from copy paper. Many times, libraries even offer bookmaking seminars for the public. For quick, functional books, I fold copy paper in half from top to bottom, make a cover from construction paper in the same way, put it together, and staple it on the fold. As you and the child complete books, you can add them to his familiar reading basket right along with the library books he is reading.

As you and the child complete books, you can add them to his familiar reading basket right along with the library books he is reading.

What to write

After the *Letter/Word Work* part of the lesson, invite the child to make up a story. Talk to the child or ask questions about one of the stories you have just read, an interesting event, a family member or pet, or something that makes him happy or sad. You should do your best to let the child come up with the story, using as much of his own wording as you can. The temptation will certainly exist to try to get him to use a new word you just practiced, or to correct his grammar. This is understandable, but you should keep your own input minimal or the child will struggle to remember what he is writing. Help him express what he wants to say, and try to monitor his story so that it will not take any more than ten minutes or so to write. If he wants to add more, suggest that he save it for tomorrow, or that you begin writing a book about the topic. The bottom line is that this is his story. You should do your best to accommodate him without your becoming the author or saying "no" too often. Once you have determined what he is going to write, record it on the lesson plan in the proper place on the left side.

Writing the story

Decide what writing instrument you will use. If you use a pencil, you can correct errors on the bottom page by simply erasing. If you use writing crayons or thin-line markers, errors can be corrected with *Post-it* white correction tape available at your local office supply store. The choice is yours, but children really enjoy picking out different colors, and the correction tape method is less messy. Sometimes, however, watercolor markers do not work well on the white tape. Trial-and-error will help you to determine what works best. I prefer using correction tape and special writing crayons that are mounted in a pen-shaped plastic tube. Rather than sharpening, the crayons are screwed out when they become dull.

Have the child repeat the story before he begins to write. Then, if he doesn't already know the first word, have him say it slowly, listening for each sound. When I talk of saying the word slowly, I do not mean in a sound-by-sound, broken up manner. Say the word as one unit but do it very slowly, stretching out the pronunciation so that the child can hear the sounds in context. In early lessons, he may hear only the first sound, or only the last sound. That's ok— help him to write the letter and then tell him what he hears in the rest of the word as you write and say it slowly. Continue this way on each word in the story. As you encounter new things, use the practice area on the top half of the writing book to work on words and letters.

Strategies to help the child record the sounds and words he hears

Depending on the word, you can use several different strategies:

Practicing letter formation

Use this as a time to practice letter formation if the child needs it. You may want to keep the alphabet book you made together nearby for reference.

Learning the word as a whole

If a word is one that would best be learned by memory, then have the child practice the word as specified in Chapter 8, writing it three or four times to gain fluency. Examples of words that fit this category are the high frequency words listed in the last chapter or ones that do not follow normal pronunciation patterns—words like *the, of, one, two, who, why, love,* or *from.* You write the word on the practice page as a model. The child then writes it himself as quickly but as neatly as possible. Have him read the word with his finger from left to right each time he writes it. Then have him write it in the story without referring to the practice page, if possible.

Word building

Story writing may provide opportunities to practice word building as described in Chapter 8. Go from what the child knows to the unknown by making logical connections. For example, if the child is writing "I like to play in the sand," you might use the child's known words to help with *like, play,* or *sand.* If he knows the name *Mike,* have him write *Mike* on the practice page and then work toward *like.* His knowledge of *day, say, may,* or *way* would be natural lead-ins to teach *play.* If he knows *and,* use this knowledge to help him write *sand.* You could do the work on the practice page or use magnetic letters on the table or on a cookie sheet.

> *Story writing may provide opportunities to practice word building . . .*

A variation of the strategy described above provides an opportunity to practice chunks like the *pl* in *play.* If the child is unfamiliar with the *pl* chunk, help him to write *play* with your assistance, telling him what he needs to know. Then discuss and write other words that start with *pl* like *plan, plane,* or *plum.* Have him write the *pl* on each one and then assist him in quickly writing the rest of the word, reading each one slowly with his finger after he writes it. The exercise could also be done with magnetic letters.

Analyzing the word—sounding it out

Words that follow general letter/sound correspondence patterns can be analyzed by the child with a little assistance from you.* Let's say that you want to work on the word *frog.* You quickly look at the word and determine that the sounds in the word are represented by letters that retain the standard sounds associated with those letters. To help the child analyze the sounds in the word, go up to the practice page and, with your pencil, make a blank line for each sound in the word. In early lessons, do not make a line for each letter—only each sound. You would make four blanks for *frog* because when the word is said slowly, each letter has a distinguishable sound. The word *like* would get three blanks because you do not hear the *e. Boat* would get three blanks because the *a* is silent:

Words that follow general letter/sound correspondence patterns can be analyzed by the child with a little assistance from you.

f r o g   l i k e   b o a t

Tell the child that he is to say the word slowly and make his finger point under each blank as he says that

*This technique is based on the work of Clay (1985) and Elkonian (1973).

sound. Remember, do not separate the sounds! Have him say them slowly in a connected voice. You will have to model this exercise for him at first. Then ask him what he hears and have him fill in the correct letter in each blank. If he makes a mistake, fix it quickly and continue. In *frog*, if he hears the *f* first, he fills it in. If the next sound that he can identify is the *g* at the end, great! Have him fill that in. Work with him until all the blanks are filled in. In the word *like*, he will not hear the *e* at the end. You just tell him that we do not hear the *e*, but it is there, and that many words have a silent *e* at the end. Then write it in. Do the same with *boat*. He will hear the *b, o,* and *t*, but you will have to tell him about the silent *a*. You will be surprised how quickly your child will learn about silent letters through this exercise. The goal is for the child to learn how to hear sounds in words, not to become "speller of the year." But this practice will help him learn proper spelling conventions because he will consistently encounter similarities in the way letters and sounds work together.

> *The goal is for the child to learn how to hear sounds in words, not to become "speller of the year."*

As the child becomes more experienced, you can tell him that now you will be making a line for each letter in the word. He will begin to make better judgments about silent letters, double consonants (like the *tt* in *butter*), or familiar chunks like *-er* or *-ing*. Do not necessarily shy away from words that have several silent letters. As long as they follow consistent patterns, you can use this exercise.

Some words to avoid in this exercise are words that have complicated groups of silent letters like *should* and *night*, words that do not have easy-to-hear sounds like *saw* and *of*, or long, complicated words like *elephant* and *ambulance*. Work on these words in alternate ways. *Should* and *night* are good word family words—talk about other *-ould* and *-ight* words. *Saw* and *of* are perfect words to have the child write several times to gain fluency by practice. On long, complicated words like *elephant* and *ambulance*, just help the child say them slowly while writing what he hears in the story on the bottom half of the practice book.

As the child works on the sentence, use opportunities to talk about capital letters or punctuation as they come up. Encourage him to do as much as he can on his own. Don't remind him ahead of time to put in a capital letter at the beginning or a period at the end. Let him remember on his own with a prompt from you only if he forgets.

When he is finished with the sentence, have him read it again from start to finish using his finger. If he is writing a book, have him do the illustrations after the lesson. Prior to writing the next day, let him read a few of his previous writings for practice and review. This will add value to his work, since you are indicating that it is worth reading again.

Some things to keep in mind

Do not let exercises drag out for long, unproductive periods of time. The child may become bored or reluctant to try new things because he doesn't want to be burdened by what he may perceive as busy work. Keep the story writing moving at a nice, smooth pace. If the child can write the word in the sentence without having to go up to the practice page, fine. Do not practice a word that the child knows well or analyze the sounds in a word if the child can quickly say it and write it on his own. Save the practice exercises for times when they will be productive.

Remember to record whatever you do on the lesson plan for future reference. Write down what you did on the practice page, and indicate on the sentence which letters the child got on his own by underlining or circling them.

Echoing words across activities establishes the connectedness of the elements of our language, and helps the child to see reading and writing as related activities that we use every day in many ways.

Encourage neatness without nagging at the child. Help him learn ways to make his words go straight across the page with the proper spacing. If making a light pencil line across the page helps him to write straight, go ahead and do it, but discontinue this practice when he can do it on his own. Show him how to make a finger space between words so that they are easier to read.

And finally, remember to make connections with the rest of the lesson whenever possible. Echoing words across activities establishes the connectedness of the elements of our language, and helps the child to see reading and writing as related activities that we use every day in many ways.

We have now covered every part of the lesson and the activities that are associated with each part. In the last chapter, we will review some important points and then put everything together by looking at elements of a sample lesson.

CHAPTER 10:
Putting It All Together:
A Sample Lesson

Some important
things to consider

Before looking at the details of a reading lesson, there are some important final points to keep in mind while working with your child. Continue reading aloud to your child. Choose books that are above her current reading level so that she is challenged by the structure of the text, the "book language" used, and the more complicated plot and details in the story. Consider reading chapter books as well, such as the *Little House* series by Laura Ingalls Wilder. Other recommendations for worthwhile reading can be found in *Honey for a Child's Heart* by Gladys Hunt (1989) or in the *Read-Aloud Handbook* by Jim Trelease mentioned in Chapter 3. For an extensive listing of children's nonfiction books, see Beverly Kobrin's *Eyeopeners II* (1995). Your read-aloud sessions should take place at a time other than the reading lesson so the child does not get too much of a good thing all at one time!

> **The best place in the lesson to work on fluency is during the time at the beginning of the lesson when she is reading familiar books.**

Model fluent reading to your child, using rising and falling pitch, changing tempo, and, of course, a smooth flow of words. Encourage her to do the same in her reading. The best place in the lesson to work on fluency is during the time at the beginning of the lesson when she is reading familiar books. Since she is reading material that is not new, this is where you can encourage her to read smoothly and with expression. It is fine to model a sentence or two and then have her try to imitate your reading. Express delight when she "reads it like a story." I often tell a child, after a particularly nice reading, that I ought to record her reading and give the tapes to other teachers to use with their classes. This and other words of encouragement will help your child to become a fluent reader, not just a person who knows how to read.

Take care to keep reading sessions as positive as possible. Find non-condemning ways to indicate errors. I've noticed that when I get obviously frustrated during a lesson, the child usually becomes demoralized or wants to quit right then and there. This can be avoided by pointing out the good things she did before drawing her attention to a problem. Try wording such as "I like the way you figured out that this is the boy's daddy, but did you notice that he doesn't call him *daddy.* Look closer at this word. It starts with an *f.*" or "You read that so well! But let's look back on page 4. This part was tricky, wasn't it?" Always remain upbeat during your lessons so that the child will look forward to them instead of dreading them. You both will be happier as a result!

If there are interruptions to the reading lesson from younger siblings, you may break the lesson into several smaller parts, coming back together as quickly as possible to maintain the continuity of ideas. It may be well just to ignore the telephone during this special time with a child.

Janet and Nicole revisited

Recall the fictional story of five-year-old Nicole and her mother Janet from Chapter 1. After a frustrating start with reading instruction, Janet was given this book by an enthusiastic friend who had put its recommendations into practice. (We'll just assume that the book wasn't available when Janet first looked into reading instruction!) Janet read the book from cover to cover in two days and decided to try to teach Nicole to read using real books. Within a week, she had purchased the necessary materials, copied the forms, and checked out the first round of picture books from the local library.

Nicole made nice initial progress in the first few weeks of their program. Janet had evaluated her knowledge of the alphabet right at the beginning and found that Nicole knew forty-eight of fifty-four upper and lower case letters. She knew most of the sounds associated with these letters as well. Janet listed all of the words Nicole knew at that point on the "Known Words" list. She could write eleven words somewhat fluently: *Nicole, mom, dad, love, a, I, see, no, go, cat,* and *me.* Since then, with Janet's patient help, she has added a few more words, including *the, and, in, we,* and *to.* Nicole is usually able to use her knowledge of these words, recognizing them when she encounters any of them in text reading. She quickly mastered the concept of one-to-one matching and is aware when her pointing does not match with what she has just read (when there are too few or too many words left at the end of the line). Nicole usually will go back when this happens to try to figure out what went wrong. Janet is currently focusing on helping Nicole use the first letter of a word to identify the word when she gets stuck, along with whatever picture (meaning) or language (grammar) cues are apparent. Sometimes Nicole even notices and uses the last

Janet is currently focusing on helping Nicole use the first letter of a word to identify the word when she gets stuck, along with whatever picture (meaning) or language (grammar) cues are apparent.

letter of a word to confirm her attempts. (Check Nicole's relative progress on the pyramid diagram at the beginning of Chapter 8.)

They usually work in the den that doubles as an office. They sit together at a desk that is wide enough for both of them. Janet sits to the right of Nicole because Janet is right-handed. This allows her to take notes on the "Lesson Plan/Journal" sheet where it is out of the way on the right side of the desk top. Just behind them is a file cabinet where they do magnetic letter work. On the table is a rectangular plastic container where Janet keeps crayon pens, white correction tape, and dry erase markers. Nicole stores her current books and her writing practice book in a plastic basket on the shelf. They get these containers and put them on the desk when it is time to read. Janet also keeps at hand a dry erase board which she bought at the local discount store.

Janet works out of a manila folder where she accumulates the lesson plans through the week.

Janet works out of a manila folder where she accumulates the lesson plans through the week. On Fridays, she transfers the lesson plan sheets to a three-ring binder. She does not work right out of the binder because it is so bulky and the rings get in the way as she tries to write. On the inside back cover of the folder Janet has stapled the "Known Words" sheet where she keeps an ever-growing list of the words that Nicole can write fluently. In the inside front of the folder, Janet keeps the "Books Read" list. Each day she writes the title of the new book that is introduced. Other

pertinent records are kept in the three-ring binder for reference when necessary.

Nicole and Janet started formal reading lessons, using
the suggestions in this book, a little over three weeks ago.
Nicole has made steady progress, and is fluently reading
books from the preprimer 1 level. Janet tries to introduce a
new book each day at the end of the lesson. To stay ahead of
where Nicole is reading and to provide wide options on
which books to use, Janet visits the library once a week.
She returns books that Nicole has mastered, renews books
that are nearly due but that she still might want to use, and
checks out a number of new books that are a level or two
above where Nicole is working. Because Janet provided the
librarian with a copy of the book list, the librarian has
kindly been requesting selections from other libraries to
keep Janet supplied with plenty of books. She also makes
recommendations of other books that are at about the same
level of difficulty. Janet has found that having as large a
selection as possible makes book choices easier each day.
She can introduce books to Nicole that are challenging, but
not overwhelming, to her blossoming literacy.

The lesson

After analyzing yesterday's lesson, Janet made a few
choices. Nicole had used the word *sand* in her writing book
and they had a somewhat fruitful discussion of how the
known word *and* was a part of *sand*. So Janet decided to
capitalize on the opportunity and work on other combina-

tions with the -*and* chunk during the Letter/Word work segment of the lesson. She decided to start with *and*, review *sand*, and then build *band, hand,* and *stand.* Janet chose the preprimer 2 book, *Five Little Ducks* by Raffi, as the new book she would introduce. She felt that Nicole was ready for the transition to the next level of difficulty and that she could easily grasp the repetitive counting pattern of the book. Also, several of Nicole's more recent books had ducks in them. This information was recorded on the lesson plan along with the title of the just-introduced new book, *I Went Walking* by Sue Williams.

Janet's completed lesson plan/journal is at the end of this chapter. You may want to refer to it as you read through the description of the lesson. Depending on your purposes and need for documentation, your plan may have more or less detail. Janet's plan/journal represents record keeping that is possibly more detailed than you need, but it is included here for your reference.

Familiar books rereading

Nicole currently has eight books in her basket that she has been able to read with a fair level of fluency. As she and Janet sit down to start the lesson, Nicole reaches into her basket and chooses three books to read: *Now We Can Go* by Ann Jonas, *Baby Says* by John Steptoe, and *Brown Bear, Brown Bear* by Bill Martin. All three of these books are at the preprimer 1 level.

Nicole picks up *Now We Can Go,* and Janet reads the title. Janet records the title and the book's level on the lesson plan sheet in the appropriate place. She does this with each familiar book Nicole reads. Nicole opens the cover and reads the title from the title page by herself. She turns the page and begins reading, using her index finger to point at the words:

"Wait a minute! I'm not ready."

Nicole turns the page and continues reading:

"I need my . . ."

She hesitates on the word *bag.* She scans the pictures for a second, looks again at the word, and then goes back to the beginning of the line:

"I need my box . . ."

Nicole hesitates again. Janet waits to say anything because she sees that Nicole is still pondering the word *bag.* Janet quickly notes on the lesson sheet that Nicole is aware of an error, and is cross-checking (pictures with text) to try to confirm her choice. The picture on the left page shows a box full of toys, while the picture on the right is of a red, empty cloth bag. Janet watches as Nicole runs her finger under the word *bag.* She mouths the /b/, then the /a/, and stops under the g. Then, as if a light comes on, Nicole says:

"Bag! I need my bag."

At this point Janet asks:

"Were you right? Is that word bag? How do you know?"

Nicole replies:

"Because I saw the g at the end."

Janet continues:

"How else did you know?"

Nicole replies:

"Because the picture shows a bag."

Janet commends Nicole on her hard work and Nicole continues reading. The whole episode took only about 20 seconds but was very helpful because it confirmed the strategies that Nicole used to correct her error. Janet makes another note on the lesson plan that Nicole had self-corrected.

Nicole reads the rest of the book without an error. Janet gives a quick positive comment about Nicole's fluent reading:

"It is fun to listen to you read that book because you read it just like the boy would have said it."

Nicole chooses *Baby Says* as her next book. Once again Janet reads the title and Nicole reads the title page. Nicole reads the books fairly quickly because the text consists of one or two words on a page. Janet decides to remove this book from Nicole's basket after the lesson because it is no longer challenging to her.

Their final familiar book is *Brown Bear, Brown Bear.* After reading the titles, Nicole starts on the first page:

"Brown bear, brown bear, what do you see?
I see a . . ."

At this point Nicole turns the page to get a preview of the next character in the story, a redbird. Janet challenges Nicole:

"Nicole, I'd like you to use what you know about words and letters to figure out what comes next without turning the page. What can you do to figure it out?"

Nicole replies almost dutifully:

"Look at the first letter and sound it."

"That's right. The first letter will help you. You might also check to see if what you try matches with the last letter of the word."

Janet records on the lesson plan that Nicole used a meaning cue, but that she prompted her to use print cues. Armed with this new challenge, Nicole continues:

"I see a redbird looking at me. (She turns the page.)

Redbird, redbird, what do you see?
I see a . . . a y-" (sounding the y in yellow)

Janet waits to see if Nicole can get the word without help. After a few seconds, Janet suggests:

"Why don't you skip that word and see if you know the next word."

Nicole goes to the next word, *duck*, and immediately recognizes it:

". . . duck, (returning to the beginning of the line) *I see a yellow duck looking at me."*

Janet seizes another teachable moment:

"Sometimes when you get stuck on a word, it helps to skip it and read on. The tricky word might pop into your head like it did for you just now. And it was good how you went back to the beginning of the line and read it again to make sure that it all sounded right."

Janet notes on the lesson plan that Nicole reread to check herself. Nicole finishes *Brown Bear* with one or two more episodes like the one above.

New book reading

At the end of the previous lesson, Janet had introduced the book *I Went Walking.* It is written in a similar format to *Brown Bear.* Janet thought it was a good choice because, as in *Brown Bear,* the pictures strongly support the text, but the verb *see* alternates with *saw* on every other page. Since Nicole knows the word *see,* she thought this book might provide an opportunity to help Nicole realize the importance of closely watching the text. Yesterday, Nicole had struggled to notice consistently the changes between *see* and *saw*. Janet was anxious to see how Nicole would do today. Janet hands Nicole the book and reminds her to watch the words closely as she reads.

After the titles, Nicole begins reading:

"I went walking. What did you see? (turn page)

I see (saw) *a black cat looking at me.* (turn page)

I went walking. What did you see? (turn page)

I see (saw) *. . . uh oh!"*

Nicole stops, looks again at the word *saw* which she had incorrectly read as *see*. Janet asks:

"What did you notice?"

With a wry little smile Nicole replies:

"That word isn't see.*"*

"What is it?"

Nicole ponders the text for a while, then shrugs her shoulders. Janet just tells her that the word is *saw* and lets her finish the book, which she does with no trouble.

When Nicole finishes, Janet commends her for her fluent reading, and for noticing that she had been reading *see* instead of *saw*. Then she turns and gets the *s*, *a*, and *w* magnetic letters and makes the word *saw* on the desk top. She says:

"This is saw. Read it."

Nicole runs her finger under the word from left to right and reads it slowly as Janet has taught her to do. Then Janet continues:

> **"Look at it closely. Now I'm going to mix it up and you make it."**

Nicole makes it thoughtfully, then reads it again with her finger. They do this again, then Janet has her write it on the dry erase board several times, reading it each time. Next, they read several lines from the book where *saw* appeared to help cement the word. Janet makes a note on the lesson plan that they practiced the word *saw* with magnetic letters and the dry erase board.

Letter/word work

Since Nicole knows a vast majority of her letters, Janet has been using this portion of the lesson to build words. She usually tries to start with a known word, and then proceeds to an unknown word. Sometimes Janet just has Nicole practice an important word by making it with magnetic letters several times like she had just done with the word *saw*. Today, they are going to build from the word *and*.

Janet asks Nicole to stand and step to the magnetic letters on the file cabinet in back of them. She gets the *a, n,* and *d* and makes the word *and*. Then she says:

> **"You know this word. Read it."**

Nicole runs her finger under the word slowly and reads it. Janet mixes up the letters, and has Nicole make it herself, which she does with no trouble. After she makes it, she automatically reads it with her finger. This is an important habit to help your child develop. It is easy to make one word after another but forget to have the child read it and look carefully at it each time. Then Janet says:

"Yesterday in your story you wrote the word sand. How do we make the word sand?"

Nicole quietly says *sand* to herself, emphasizing the first letter.

"Sssssand. I hear the s."

Janet picks up the letter *s* and hands it to Nicole.

"You make it say sand."

Nicole places the *s* in front of the *-and* and then reads it with her finger. Janet slides the *s* to the left side a few inches from the *-and* chunk.

"Now say band. (Nicole does so.) **How do we make band?"**

"We need to put a b on the front."

Janet gets the *b*, hands it to Nicole, and watches her place it in front of *-and*, making *band*. Nicole reads it. Janet slides the *b* to the left and puts it under the *s*.

"How would we make hand? You make it say hand."

Nicole pauses for a moment. *H* is one of Nicole's less-fluent letters. Nicole says *hand* several times very slowly, but she just can't seem to recall the letter that goes with the /h/ sound. Janet has been using a simple hand motion to help Nicole remember—she puts her open hand in front of her mouth and says:

"H-h-hand." (making puffing /h/ sounds)

Nicole watches her, does the same, and immediately says:

"H! It's h . . . hand."

Without prompting her to do so, Nicole reaches for the letter *h*, puts it in front of *-and,* and reads *hand* slowly with her finger. Janet says:

"You are right. It is h."

Janet slides the *h* to the left under the other two letters. She continues:

"Now I have one more. Listen carefully and watch my mouth. Stand . . . stand. You say it. How would we make stand?"

Nicole says *stand* slowly and thoughtfully. She looks at the letter *s* to the left of the *-and* chunk, then she slides it over in front of the chunk. Nicole quietly says *stand* to herself several times as she studies the word she just made. Then she turns to Janet and says:

"I hear a t."

"You are right. You do hear a t. Where is the t?"

While Nicole is thinking, Janet picks up the letter *t*. Nicole says *stand* again.

"I hear the t *after the* s.*"*

Janet hands the *t* to Nicole and says:

"Make it say stand."

Nicole places the *t* just after the *s* and reads it slowly. Janet gives her a big hug and says:

"You really were thinking hard on that one! Great work! I'm going to slide the s and the t back over here. Now I will say the word and you make it by moving the letter."

At this point, the letters are arranged like this:

s

b

h   **-and**

t

Janet says *sand*. Nicole moves the correct letter from the left to the position in front of the chunk. She reads it with her finger, then slides it back. This is repeated with each word. Then Janet says:

"Now you move the letter and tell me the word."

Nicole goes through each word once more, moving the letter(s) herself, reading the word, and sliding the letter(s) back to the left. Janet asks Nicole to sit down at the desk beside her. She hands the dry erase board and a marker to Nicole and says:

"Make the letter h here. Make it again . . . and again."

Each time Nicole makes the letter, she says its name. Janet did this just to provide one more bit of practice on the difficult letter at a time when it would be meaningful. Janet puts a check mark beside each word (*and, sand, band, hand, stand*) that she had written on the lesson plan indicating that they had actually worked on the word. Janet also adds a note that they practiced the letter *h*.

Story writing

As Janet gets Nicole's writing practice book out of the basket she says:

"I really enjoyed the book we read a little bit ago, I Went Walking. What was your favorite part?"

"The duck part. I like ducks. I saw a duck today."

"You did? And where was this duck?"

"By the lake at Mrs. Clark's house. When Daddy and I took a walk it was there, but it ran into the water when we got close."

"Let's write about that duck. What do you want to say about it?"

Nicole thinks for a moment. She is pondering the words she wants to use. Then she says:

"We saw a duck by the lake."

"That sounds good, Nicole. Say it one more time so I can write it down."

Janet asks Nicole to repeat her sentence so that it will be easier for her to remember as she is writing, and to give her time to record Nicole's sentence on the lesson plan. Janet is happy because Nicole used the word *saw* which is the word they had practiced earlier.

Janet opens the writing practice book to the next clear two-page spread. Recall that the book is made from copy paper bound on the long side. Nicole will write her sentence on the bottom half of the book and use the top half for practice. Janet writes the date on the top right corner of the practice page.

She hands the green crayon pen to Nicole and says:

"You know the word we. Go ahead and write we."

Nicole quickly writes the word. She looks at Janet. Janet gives her one of those looks that is intended to let Nicole know that something isn't quite right. Janet says:

"That word is we. But I'm thinking about how this is the first word of your sentence."

"Oh, I forgot. I need a capital W."

Janet uses a piece of white correction tape to cover the *w*. Nicole writes a capital *W* on top of the tape. Nicole says:

"We . . . saw. I need to write saw. *Ssssaw. S!"*

Nicole proceeds to write an *s* after measuring a finger-width space after the word *we*. Janet told her to do this to help her with spacing between words. Janet is pleased that Nicole is taking on so much of the writing task herself. Nicole says the word several times to try to hear other sounds.

"Saw . . . saw . . . I don't know what's next."

"Nicole, do you remember that we read this word in I Went Walking? You also made it with magnetic letters and wrote it a few times."

"Oh, yeah."

"Write saw up here. Just write what you remember."

Nicole goes up to the practice page and slowly writes *s - o - w*. She runs her finger under the word and reads:

"Saw."

"You do hear what sounds like an o in the middle. But this word is different. That middle letter is an a. (Janet takes the pen and changes the *o* to an *a*.) **It's a word that you just have to remember. I'm glad that you did remember the w at the end. Write saw in each corner for practice."**

Nicole does so, reading the word each time she writes it. Then she writes it in the story.

"We saw a . . . I can write a (she does). We saw a duck . . . duck . . . /d/ . . . /d/"

She writes a *d* in the book after pondering how a lower case *d* is made. As the writing is proceeding, Janet has been making notations on the lesson plan. She underlined *We* with an unbroken line indicating that Nicole wrote the whole word herself. The *s* and *w* in *saw* are underlined individually which shows that Nicole wrote those letters. Janet also underlines the word *a*, and she underlines the *d* in *duck*. She made a note on the right that they talked about capital letters at the beginning of sentences, and that Nicole practiced writing *saw* on the practice page. Now Janet has made a decision about how to help Nicole with the word *duck*.

Janet uses her pencil and makes three blank lines on the practice page, leaving a little bit of space between the blanks:

_____   _____   _____

Then she said:

"Say duck very slowly and point at a blank line for each sound you hear, like this."

Janet demonstrates. She takes the crayon pen from Nicole and encourages her to do the same. Nicole slowly says the word and deliberately moves her finger in a looping fashion, pointing at each blank. She points back at the first line.

"/D/. This is a d."

Janet hands her the pen and Nicole puts a *d* on the first line. She points and says *duck* again.

"Duck . . . /k/. . . /k/. This last one is k."

Nicole fills in a *k.* Janet has drawn the lines on her lesson plan and is circling the letters that Nicole is getting on her own. Nicole continues:

"Duck, duck. /U/ . . . /u/ . . . umbrella. (Nicole's anchor word for the /u/ is *umbrella.) This middle one is* u."

"Yes, Nicole! You really listened carefully on that one. It is a u."

Nicole fills in the *u* on the middle line. Janet continues:

"There is one more letter that we don't hear in this word. There is a c right here between the u and the k. A lot of words end with this -ck chunk."

Janet decides to save a discussion about the *-ck* chunk for another day. She could have written several words ending with *-ck* on the practice page, or she could have found more *-ck* words in some of Nicole's familiar books. But a quick check of the clock indicated to Janet that it would be best just to move along. She told Nicole to finish writing *duck* in her story.

"We saw a duck by . . . by . . . b."

Nicole writes the *b* in her story. She ponders the next letter:

"By . . . by . . . it sounds like i.*"*

"Yes it does, Nicole. But . . . I'll tell you what. You know the word my. Write my up here on your practice page. (Nicole does.) **Read it.** (Nicole does.) **Now think, how would we make by?"**

Nicole ponders the word *my.* Then she says *by.* Then she writes a *b* in front of the word *my* and reads:

"By."

"Do we need that m?"

Nicole quickly realizes that she doesn't. With a giggle she puts an *x* on the *m*, then she writes *by* underneath it. Janet tells her to write *by* a few more times for practice. On her lesson plan Janet writes *my;* then she draws a short arrow and writes *by*, indicating that she used one word to lead to the other. She also noted that Nicole practiced writing *by*. Nicole writes *by* in the story and continues:

"We saw a duck by the . . . the."

Nicole quickly writes *the* in her story. It is a word they have practiced and read many times.

"We saw a duck by the lake . . . lake . . . l."

Nicole fills in the *l*. She is able to hear the *a* and the *k* in the same way and she writes them in as well.

"Lake! That's all!"

"Well, not quite. There is a letter we don't hear at the end."

Almost before Janet could finish, Nicole calls out "*E!*" They have already encountered the silent e many times in their reading and writing. Nicole fills in the *e* at the end of *lake* and then reads the entire sentence with her finger.

"We saw a duck by the lake."

"Are we finished?"

"Nope. We put a period at the end."

Janet has Nicole read the sentence one more time for practice and finishes some final notations on the lesson plan. Janet quickly flips back to the previous day's story and has Nicole read that as well. She points out the word *sand*, reminding Nicole that they made it and some similar words with magnetic letters just a little earlier. Now they are ready for the final part of the lesson.

New book introduction

The new book Janet has chosen to introduce today is Raffi's *Five Little Ducks*. It has repeating text that follows a backward counting pattern:

Five little ducks went out one day,
Over the hills and far away.
Mother Duck said, "Quack, quack, quack, quack,"
But only four little ducks came back.

In planning for the lesson, Janet had written some notes about her introduction. She wanted to use the same wording that appears in the book, including words like *went, over, far away, Mother Duck,* and *came back.* She also noted that she would have Nicole locate two new and somewhat unfamiliar words prior to reading, *sad* and *none.* She felt that Nicole would grasp most of the other words simply because they were repeated so often, but *sad* and *none* were important words in the story that only appeared once.

As Janet puts Nicole's writing book back in her basket she says:

> **"We've been reading several books about ducks lately. Here is another one called Five Little Ducks. Each day the ducks went over the hills and far away."**

Janet shows Nicole the cover and begins turning the pages slowly as Nicole looks on. She is using much of the wording from the story to familiarize Nicole with the vocabulary.

> **"That mother duck said 'Quack,' but not all the ducks came back."**

"Why not?"

> **"Well, what do you think? You look at the pictures and see if you can figure out why."**

Nicole continues turning the pages on her own. On one of the pages, the despondent mother duck is in the rain with a sad look on her face. Janet remarks:

"There is Mother Duck. She looks sad. None of her ducks came back. Nicole, say none. (Nicole does.) *What letter is at the beginning of none?"*

"N?"

"Yes, you do hear an N. Now find none."

Of course, Janet made sure that the word *none* is on the page they are looking at. Nicole scans the text, locates *none*, and reads it with her finger. They turn the pages, and Janet repeats the above process with the word *sad.* They continue discussing the story, noting that the seasons change, and that the ducks must have remained away for a long time. Janet asks:

"I wonder where those five little ducks went?"

"Maybe they grew up."

"Do you think so? Oh look, Mother Duck said 'Quack, quack' again. I wonder if they will come back now."

Nicole turns the page to reveal the five little ducks making a triumphant return with their families following. Nicole remarks:

"They all came back with their babies!"

"Yes, and they must have gotten married because there are their mates. I like happy endings! Now let's go back to the beginning and you can read."

Janet is satisfied with the first introduction because Nicole had a chance to hear and/or use most of the words in the story at least once. She feels that Nicole will be able to use what she knows about the story and about how words work to read it rather successfully.

They go back to the beginning and they read the title again. Nicole starts on the first page:

"Five . . . little . . . ducks went out one day,

O . . . over the hill (hills) *and far away."*

Janet decides not to comment at this point on the error where Nicole ignored the *s* on *hills*. She will wait to see if Nicole fixes it herself as the text repeats. Nicole turns the page:

"Mother Duck says . . . (Nicole shakes her head) *. . . said . . . 'Quack, quack, quack, quack."*

Janet decides to jump in:

"You changed says **to** said. **Why?"**

"I saw the d.*"*

"I'm glad you noticed. Good readers always watch to make sure that what they say and what they see match."

Janet writes on the lesson plan that Nicole self-corrected, using print cues. Nicole turns the page:

"B . . . b . . . ba . . . t, bat only four little ducks came back."

Nicole hesitates. Janet asks:

"What is the matter?"

"Something doesn't sound right."

"Where is the tricky part?"

"This b word."

"You are right, Nicole. It doesn't sound right to say 'Bat only four little ducks came back.' We don't talk that way. What would sound right that looks like this word?"

Nicole still is stumped. Janet thinks of another approach. She gets the dry erase board and hands a marker to Nicole:

"You know cat. Write cat. (Nicole does). **Now how would you make bat?"**

Nicole erases the *c* and replaces it with a *b*. Then she reads it. Janet takes the marker and says:

"Yes, this is bat. Now I will change the middle letter to u like it is in the story. How does the letter u sound."

"/U/ . . . /u/ . . . umbrella."

"Let's sound through this word together."

Janet points as they sound through the word, slowly connecting all the letter sounds.

"But! But only four little ducks came back."

"Great! I'm glad that you noticed that the sentence didn't sound right and you stopped. Go ahead."

Nicole continues as the pattern repeats. Janet notes on the lesson plan that Nicole was aware of an error because of grammar cues. She also noted that they went from *cat* to *bat* to *but* using the dry erase board.

Janet watches to see if Nicole changes the word *hill* to *hills* as she continues reading. Nicole does, so Janet will not mention her initial error. Nicole reads the balance of the book fairly smoothly, stopping momentarily to think before reading the word *none*. Because they had found it during the introduction, Nicole was able to use the context of the story and the first letter to figure it out.

Don't worry about making mistakes. If you are positive, purposeful, and consistent, you will help your child to become a confident reader.

Janet decides that there is no need to read through the story again. The text repeats enough that Nicole should be able to piece together cues from all three sources to read it again tomorrow with little help from Janet. She is pleased with her choice of this book. It provided a smooth transition to the preprimer 2 level. The lesson lasted about 35 minutes and was very productive. Janet thanks Nicole for working so hard and sends her out to play. She spends the next few minutes looking over the lesson and making plans for tomorrow.

Practice makes perfect

You may be thinking that you could never make the choices "on the run" that Janet did. But as you start in, and as you constantly review the information in this book, you will become confident in the methodology. Remember that Janet's choices weren't the only ones that could have been made. She had several different options about how to handle the teaching opportunities that presented themselves. Don't worry about making mistakes. If you are positive, purposeful, and consistent, you will help your child to become a confident reader.

There should come a time when you notice that the child seems to blossom in her abilities. She will become a real problem solver as she reads.

If possible, begin this program as a partner with another parent or tutor, or find someone who has used the same techniques to teach a child to read. Talk to a teacher at your local school—one who is experienced in literature-based teaching or is trained in Reading Recovery. Ask him/her for ideas when you seem to have problems. Share what has worked for you and where you want to go next. It is easy to get into a rut when you are doing it alone.

There should come a time when you notice that the child seems to blossom in her abilities. She will become a real problem solver as she reads. She will want to do more reading on her own. This will be the time when you can change direction in your program. You will want to spend more time talking about the plot, characters, and lessons in the stories you read and less time working through the mechanics of print. At that point, your child will have "graduated" from this program! Talk to your home schooling friends or another teacher about the direction you should take next. And give yourself a big pat on the back! You taught a child to read using real books!

Lesson Plan/Journal

Child's Name ___Nicole___ Date ___9/26/95___

Activity	Observations/Teaching Points

Familiar Books Rereading

Titles:
Now We Can Go (PP1)
Baby Says (PP1)
Brown Bear, Brown Bear (PP1)

- aware of error
- cross checking
- self correction
- using M cues/ prompt to P cues
- reread to check

New Book Reading (introduced at end of last lesson)

Title: I Went Walking (PP1)

- aware of error
- practiced saw w/ mag. letters and dry erase

Letter/Word Work

Letter(s) or Word(s): and ✔ hand ✔
sand ✔ stand ✔
band ✔

- practiced h with dry erase

Story writing

Sentence: We saw a duck
by the lake.

- talked about capital at beginning of sentence
- practiced saw
- ⓓ ⓤ c ⓚ
- mentioned -ck chunk
- my ⟶ by
- practiced by

New Book Introduction

Title: Five Little Ducks (PP2)

Introduction: - phrasing - went, over, far away,
mother duck, came back
- locate sad and none

- self corrected using P cues
- aware of error using G cues
- cat ⟶ bat ⟶ but

APPENDIX A:
A Bibliography of Children's Trade Books

About this booklist

The term "trade books" defines children's books that are written for the edification and enjoyment of children. Included in this list are just some of the many books that you can use in teaching your child to read. Nearly all of these books are still in print and many can be found at your local library. They also can be ordered from bookstores if you wish. They are in approximate levels of increasing difficulty based on the reading levels used in most schools. But remember, a book's difficulty is relative, based on the individual child and his unique experiences. I have seen children who could not otherwise read even the simplest story pick up a book filled with multisyllabic dinosaur names and read it fluently without hesitation. What your child will find easy or difficult will sometimes perplex and amaze you!

I have compiled this list of books based on my own training and experience in teaching children to read. Many of these books are used in the Reading Recovery® program. I have also used the recommendations of other teachers who are knowledgeable about early literacy and learning to read.

The more than 600 books in this list represent a wide range of topics that are familiar to most children. Many of them are about realistic situations, and many are based in fantasy. I cannot predict which books you may find objectionable in sharing with your child. This will need to be your call. One person may not like a book that has monsters, witches, or fairies, but these things may not bother the next. The rule of thumb is this: never use a book with a child that you have not previewed yourself. Of course, to introduce a new book correctly, you will need to familiarize yourself with the elements of the story, the vocabulary, and the pattern used. At that time you can determine the appropriateness of the book's content for use in your program.

These books will be in the children's picture book section filed alphabetically by the author's last name. The levels I used in classifying them are the ones used in most public and private school systems. I have given very general descriptions of the books in each level to assist you in choosing the appropriate books for your child.

Author's note: I recommend going to your local library to get books on this list, or comparable ones. However, if your local library does not have the ones you want and you cannot get them through inter-library loan, you may want to consider buying a few for your home collection. The following organizations are good sources for inexpensive children's books:

Chinaberry Book Service, 2780 Via Orange Way, Suite B, Spring Valley, CA 91978
 1-800-776-2242

Michaels Associates, 4332 Old William Penn Hwy., Monroeville, PA 15146
 1-800-869-1467

LEVEL E: Emergent Literacy

The books in this level use topics and language familiar to young children who are becoming aware of print. The text is minimal, is often repetitive, and is very descriptive of the pictures.

AUTHOR(S)	TITLE	YEAR	PUBLISHER
Aruego, Jose	*Look What I Can Do*	1988	Lothrop
Carle, Eric	*Do You Want to Be My Friend?*	1971	Crowell
Carle, Eric	*Have You Seen My Cat?*	1987	Picture Book Studio
Gomi, Taro	*Where's the Fish?*	1977	Morrow
Hoban, Tana	*Count and See*	1972	Greenwillow
Hoff, Syd	*Barney's Horse*	1990	Harper
Hutchins, Pat	*1 Hunter*	1982	Greenwillow
Maris, Ron	*My Book*	1983	Viking
Mayer, Mercer	*Oops*	1977	Dial Press
McMillan, Bruce	*Growing Colors*	1988	Lothrop, Lee, & Shepard
Pienkowski, Jan	*Colors*	1989	Simon & Schuster
Pienkowski, Jan	*Shapes*	1989	Simon & Schuster
Tafuri, Nancy	*Have You Seen My Duckling?*	1984	Puffin
Wildsmith, Brian	*Applebird*	1987	Oxford
Wildsmith, Brian	*Cat on the Mat*	1987	Oxford
Ziefert, Harriet	*Mommy, Where Are You?*	1988	Puffin
Ziefert, Harriet	*Where Is My Dinner?*	1984	Grosset & Dunlap
Ziefert, Harriet	*Where Is My Friend?*	1984	Grosset & Dunlap

LEVELS PP1, PP2, and PP3: Preprimers

Preprimer books are used in schools to teach the basics of reading text. They are the children's first readers, and they are usually encountered late in kindergarten and during the first part of first grade. Books in the preprimer levels use many high-frequency words and have repetitive patterns that are very predictable. The pictures strongly support the text. The subject matter, vocabulary, and language patterns are very familiar to young children.

The amount of text and the difficulty increase from the preprimer 1 to the preprimer 2 and 3 levels. The books will become less repetitive and predictable, and the pictures will tell less of the story than in earlier levels.

LEVEL PP1: Preprimer 1

AUTHOR(S)	TITLE	YEAR	PUBLISHER
Eberts, Marjorie	*Pancakes, Crackers, and Pizza*	1984	Children's Press
Gregorich, Barbara	*Fox on the Box*	1984	School Zone
Gregorich, Barbara	*I Want a Pet*	1984	School Zone
Jonas, Ann	*Now We Can Go*	1986	Greenwillow
Kalan, Robert	*Rain*	1978	Greenwillow
Martin, Bill	*Brown Bear/What Do You See?*	1984	Holt, Rinehart, Winston
Minarik, Else H.	*It's Spring!*	1989	Greenwillow
Mueller, Virginia	*Halloween Mask for Monster*	1986	Whitman
Mueller, Virginia	*A Playhouse for Monster*	1985	Whitman
Peek, Merle	*Roll Over*	1981	Clarion
Petrie, Catherine	*Joshua James Likes Trucks*	1982	Children's Press
Sawicki, Norma J.	*The Little Red House*	1989	Lothrop, Lee, & Shepard
Steptoe, John	*Baby Says*	1988	Morrow
Stobbs, William	*Gregory's Dog*	1987	Oxford
Tafuri, Nancy	*Spots, Feathers, and Curly Tails*	1988	Greenwillow
Tafuri, Nancy	*Who's Counting?*	1986	Greenwillow
Wildsmith, Brian	*All Fall Down*	1983	Oxford
Wildsmith, Brian	*Toot, Toot*	1984	Oxford
Wildsmith, Brian	*What a Tale*	1987	Oxford
Williams, Sue	*I Went Walking*	1990	HBJ
Wood, Leslie	*Frog and the Fly*	1987	Oxford
Ziefert, Harriet	*Where Is My Baby?*	1994	Harper

LEVEL PP2: Preprimer 2

AUTHOR(S)	TITLE	YEAR	PUBLISHER
Antle, Nancy	*Good Bad Cat*	1985	School Zone
Barton, Bryon	*Where's Al?*	1972	Seaburty Press
Berenstain, Jan and Stan	*Bears in the Night*	1971	Random House
Berenstain, Jan and Stan	*Bears on Wheels*	1969	Random House
Browne, Anthony	*I Like Books*	1988	Knopf
Browne, Anthony	*Things I Like*	1989	Knopf
Carter, David A.	*How Many Bugs in a Box?*	1988	Simon & Schuster
Ginsburg, Mirra	*Chick and Duckling*	1972	Simon & Schuster
Greene, Carol	*Ice Is—Whee!*	1983	Children's Press
Greene, Carol	*Snow Joe*	1982	Children's Press
Greydanus, Rose	*Freddie the Frog*	1980	Troll Associates
Hamsa, Bobbie	*Dirty Larry*	1983	Children's Press
Hamsa, Bobbie	*Fast Draw Freddie*	1984	Children's Press
Hellard, Susan	*This Little Piggy*	1989	Putnam
Jones, Carol	*Old MacDonald Had a Farm*	1989	Houghton Mifflin
Lewison, Wendy	*Mud*	1990	Random House
Lillegard, Dee	*Where Is It?*	1984	Children's Press

Lindgren, Barbro	Sam's Ball	1983	Morrow
Lindgren, Barbro	Sam's Cookie	1982	Morrow
Lindgren, Barbro	Sam's Lamp	1983	Morrow
Lindgren, Barbro	Sam's Teddy Bear	1982	Morrow
Lindgren, Barbro	Sam's Wagon	1986	Morrow
Mark, Jan	Fur	1986	Harper
Matthias, Catherine	Too Many Balloons	1982	Children's Press
Mueller, Virginia	Monster and the Baby	1985	Whitman
Mueller, Virginia	Monster Can't Sleep	1988	Puffin
Peek, Merle	Mary Wore Her Red Dress	1993	Houghton Mifflin
Poulet, Virgnina	Blue Bug Goes to School	1985	Children's Press
Raffi	Five Little Ducks	1989	Crown
Rounds, Glen	Old MacDonald Had a Farm	1989	Holiday House
Sharp, Paul	Paul the Pitcher	1984	Children's Press
Stobbs, William	One, Two, Buckle My Shoe	1984	Bodley, Head
Tafuri, Nancy	Ball Bounced	1989	Greenwillow
Watanabe, Shigeo	I Can Build a House!	1983	Philomel
Wildsmith, Brian	Animal Shapes	1980	Oxford
Wylie, Joanne and David	Fishy Color Story	1983	Children's Press
Wylie, Joanne and David	Funny Fish Story	1984	Children's Press

LEVEL PP3: Preprimer 3

AUTHOR(S)	TITLE	YEAR	PUBLISHER
Adams, Pam	There Were Ten in the Bed	1979	Child's Play
Berenstain, Jan and Stan	Inside, Outside, Upside Down	1969	Random House
Burningham, John	Blanket	1975	Crowell
Burningham, John	School	1975	Crowell
Campbell, Rod	Henry's Busy Day	1984	Viking
Christelow, Eileen	Five Little Monkeys Jumping on the Bed	1993	Houghton Mifflin
Crews, Donald	Flying	1986	Greenwillow
Eastman, P.D.	Go Dog Go	1961	Beginner Books
Fehlner, C.	Dog and Cat	1990	Children's Press
Greene, Carol	Hi, Clouds	1983	Children's Press
Gregorich, Barbara	Gum on the Drum	1984	School Zone
Grey, Judith	Mud Pies	1981	Troll
Hamsa, Bobbie	Animal Babies	1985	Children's Press
Hill, Eric	Where's Spot?	1988	Interlink
Jonas, Ann	Where Can It Be?	1986	Greenwillow
Kowalczyk, Carolyn	Purple Is Part of the Rainbow	1985	Children's Press
Kraus, Robert	Herman the Helper	1987	Simon & Schuster
Langstaff, John	Oh, A-Hunting We Will Go	1974	Atheneum
Matthias, Catherine	I Love Cats	1983	Children's Press
Matthias, Catherine	Out the Door	1982	Children's Press
Mayer, Mercer	All By Myself	1985	Western Publishing
McDaniel, Becky B.	Katie Did It	1983	Children's Press
McKissack, Patricia	Who Is Who?	1983	Children's Press
Neasi, Barbara	Just Like Me	1984	Children's Press
Parkinson, Kathy	Farmer in the Dell	1988	Whitman
Perkins, Al	Ear Book	1968	Random House
Perkins, Al	Nose Book	1970	Random House
Petrie, Catherine	Hot Rod Harry	1982	Children's Press

Level PP3 continued

Poulet, Virginia	*Blue Bug's Book of Colors*	1981	Children's Press
Roffey, Maureen	*Home Sweet Home*	1982	Bodley Head
Seuss, Dr.	*Foot Book*	1968	Random House
Shaw, Charles G.	*It Looked Like Spilt Milk*	1993	Harper
Snow, Pegeen	*Eat Your Peas, Louise!*	1985	Children's Press
Wildsmith, Brian	*Island*	1987	Oxford
Wylie, Joanne and David	*More or Less Fish Story*	1984	Children's Press

LEVEL P: Primer

Children are usually reading primer level books in the second or third quarter of the first grade year. As you can imagine, these books still use familiar language, but the illustrations only provide moderate support. Much less repetitive language is used, although the stories still retain a fair amount of predictability.

AUTHOR(S)	TITLE	YEAR	PUBLISHER
Adams, Pam	*This Old Man*	1974	Child's Play
Ahlberg, Janet and Allan	*Each Peach Pear Plum*	1986	Puffin Books
Asch, Frank	*Just Like Daddy*	1984	Simon & Schuster
Bang, Molly	*Ten, Nine, Eight*	1983	Greenwillow
Barton, Byron	*Dinosaurs, Dinosaurs*	1989	Harper
Blocksma, Mary	*Apple Tree, Apple Tree*	1983	Children's Press
Bonsall, Crosby N.	*Day I Had to Play with My Sister*	1972	Harper
Bonsall, Crosby N.	*Mine's the Best*	1973	Harper
Brandenberg, Franz	*Cock-a-Doodle Do*	1986	Greenwillow
Brandenberg, Franz	*I Wish I Was Sick Too*	1976	Greenwillow
Brown, Ruth	*A Dark Dark Tale*	1981	Dial Press
Burningham, John	*Baby*	1975	Crowell
Burningham, John	*Cupboard*	1975	Crowell
Burningham, John	*Dog*	1975	Crowell
Burningham, John	*Friend*	1975	Crowell
Burningham, John	*Snow*	1974	Crowell
Campbell, Rod	*Dear Zoo*	1986	Simon & Schuster
Campbell, Rod	*Oh Dear!*	1986	Fourwinds Press
Craig, Janet	*Here Comes Winter*	1988	Troll
Craig, Janet	*Little Danny Dinosaur*	1988	Troll
Crews, Donald	*Ten Black Dots*	1986	Greenwillow
Damon, Laura	*Secret Valentine*	1988	Troll
DeRegniers, Beatrice S.	*Going for a Walk*	1993	Harper
Dijis, Carla	*Are You My Daddy?*	1990	Simon & Schuster
Dijis, Carla	*Are You My Mommy?*	1990	Simon & Schuster
Dorros, Arthur	*Alligator Shoes*	1982	Duton
Doyle, R.H.	*Freddie's Spaghetti*	1991	Random House
Eastman, Patricia	*Sometimes Things Change*	1983	Children's Press
Galdone, Paul	*Cat Goes Fiddle-I-Fee*	1988	Houghton Mifflin

Gelman, Rita G.	*More Spaghetti I Say*	1993	Scholastic
Gelman, Rita G.	*Why Can't I Fly?*	1986	Scholastic
Gerstein, Mordicai	*Roll Over*	1988	Crown
Gerstein, Mordicai	*William, Where Are You?*	1985	Crown
Ginsburg, Mirra	*Across the Stream*	1982	Greenwillow
Ginsburg, Mirra	*Three Kittens*	1973	Crown
Goor, Ron and Nancy	*Signs*	1983	Crowell
Gordon, Sharon	*Christmas Surprise*	1980	Troll
Gordon, Sharon	*Easter Bunny's Lost Egg*	1980	Troll
Gordon, Sharon	*Friendly Snowman*	1980	Troll
Gordon, Sharon	*Home for a Puppy*	1988	Troll
Gordon, Sharon	*Mike's First Haircut*	1988	Troll
Gordon, Sharon	*Pete the Parakeet*	1980	Troll
Gordon, Sharon	*Show and Tell*	1988	Troll
Gordon, Sharon	*Three Little Witches*	1980	Troll
Gordon, Sharon	*What a Dog*	1980	Troll
Greene, Carol	*Shine, Sun!*	1983	Children's Press
Gregorich, Barbara	*Beep, Beep*	1984	School Zone
Gregorich, Barbara	*Jog Frog Jog*	1984	School Zone
Gregorich, Barbara	*My Friend Goes Left*	1984	School Zone
Gregorich, Barbara	*Sue Likes Blue*	1984	School Zone
Gregorich, Barbara	*Up Went the Goat*	1984	School Zone
Greydanus, Rose	*Animals at the Zoo*	1980	Troll
Greydanus, Rose	*Big Red Fire Engine*	1980	Troll
Greydanus, Rose	*Mike's New Bike*	1980	Troll
Greydanus, Rose	*My Secret Hiding Place*	1980	Troll
Greydanus, Rose	*Susie Goes Shopping*	1980	Troll
Greydanus, Rose	*Tree House Fun*	1980	Troll
Greydanus, Rose	*Willie the Slowpoke*	1980	Troll
Hellen, Nancy	*Bus Stop*	1988	Orchard
Henkes, Kevin	*SHHHH*	1989	Greenwillow
Hennessy, B.G.	*Missing Tarts*	1970	Viking Kestrel
Hill, Eric	*Spot's First Wall*	1986	Putnam
Hurd, Edith T.	*Johnny Lion's Rubber Boots*	1972	Harper
Hutchins, Pat	*Rosie's Walk*	1968	Macmillan
Hutchins, Pat	*Titch*	1973	Macmillan
Johnson, Mildred	*Wait, Skates!*	1983	Children's Press
Johnson, Sharon S.	*I Want to Be a Clown*	1985	School Zone
Jonas, Ann	*When You Were a Baby*	1982	Greenwillow
Keller, Holly	*Ten Sleepy Sheep*	1983	Greenwillow
Kline, Suzy	*Shhhh!*	1984	Whitman
Kraus, Robert	*Boris Is Bad Enough*	1988	Simon & Schuster
Kraus, Robert	*Herman the Helper Lends a Hand*	1981	Windmill
Kraus, Ruth	*Carrot Seed*	1989	Harper
Lloyd, David	*Grandma and the Pirate*	1985	Crown
Long, Earlene R.	*Gone Fishing*	1987	Houghton Mifflin
Mack, Stan	*Ten Bears in My Bed*	1974	Pantheon
Maris, Ron	*Are You There, Bear?*	1985	Greenwillow
Maris, Ron	*Is Anyone Home?*	1984	Greenwillow
Mayer, Mercer	*Just For You*	1975	Golden Press
Mayer, Mercer	*Just Me and My Babysitter*	1986	Western
McDaniel, Becky B.	*Katie Couldn't*	1985	Children's Press
Minarik, Else H.	*Cat and Dog*	1960	Harper
Oxenbury, Helen	*Say Goodnight*	1987	Simon & Schuster
Peters, Sharon	*Happy Jack*	1980	Troll
Peters, Sharon	*Messy Mark*	1980	Troll
Peters, Sharon	*Puppet Show*	1980	Troll

Level P continued

Peters, Sharon	*Ready, Get Set, Go!*	1980	Troll
Peters, Sharon	*Stop That Rabbit*	1980	Troll
Peters, Sharon	*Tiny Christmas Elf*	1988	Troll
Peters, Sharon	*Trick or Treat Halloween*	1980	Troll
Phillips, Joan	*My New Boy*	1986	Random House
Phillips, Joan	*Tiger Is a Scaredy Cat*	1986	Random House
Raffi	*Wheels on the Bus*	1988	Crown
Reese, Bob	*Critter Race*	1981	Children's Press
Reese, Bob	*Huzzard Buzzard*	1981	Children's Press
Reese, Bob	*Scary Larry*	1981	Children's Press
Reese, Bob	*Tweedle-De-Dee Tumbleweed*	1981	Children's Press
Rockwell, Anne	*Boats*	1993	Puffin Books
Rockwell, Anne	*Cars*	1984	Dutton
Rockwell, Harlow	*My Kitchen*	1980	Greenwillow
Schneider, Rex	*That's Not All*	1985	School Zone
Shaw, Nancy	*Sheep in a Jeep*	1986	Houghton Mifflin
Shulevitz, Uri	*One Monday Morning*	1974	Simon & Schuster
Simon, Shirley	*Foolish Goose*	1985	School Zone
Stadler, John	*Hooray for Snail!*	1984	Harper
Stadler, John	*Snail Saves the Day*	1985	Harper
Stadler, John	*Three Cheers for Hippo*	1987	Crowell
Stobbs, William	*Gregory's Garden*	1987	Oxford
Taylor, Judy	*My Dog*	1987	Macmillan
Testa, Fulvio	*If You Take a Paintbrush*	1982	Dial Press
Van Laan, Nancy	*Big Fat Worm*	1987	Knopf
Ward, Cindy	*Cookie's Week*	1988	Putnam
Watanabe, Shigeo	*I'm King of the Castle!*	1982	Philomel
Watanabe, Shigeo	*Where's My Daddy?*	1982	Philomel
Watson, Wendy	*Lollipop*	1976	Crowell
West, Colin	*Have You Seen the Crocodile?*	1987	Harper
West, Colin	*"Not Me," Said the Monkey*	1987	Harper
West, Colin	*Pardon? Said the Giraffe*	1986	Harper
Westcott, Nadine B.	*Lady with the Alligator Purse*	1988	Little, Brown
Westcott, Nadine B.	*Peanut Butter and Jelly*	1987	Dutton
Wheeler, Cindy	*Marmalade's Nap*	1982	Knopf
Wheeler, Cindy	*Marmalade's Snowy Day*	1983	Knopf
Wheeler, Cindy	*Rose*	1985	Knopf
Wylie, Joanne and David	*Fishy Alphabet Story*	1983	Children's Press
Ziefert, Harriet	*Harry Takes a Bath*	1987	Puffin Books
Ziefert, Harriet	*Here Comes the Bus*	1988	Penguin
Ziefert, Harriet	*Jason's Bus Ride*	1989	Viking
Ziefert, Harriet	*Later, Rover*	1991	Viking
Ziefert, Harriet	*Mike and Tony: Best Friends*	1987	Viking
Ziefert, Harriet	*New House for Mole and Mouse*	1987	Viking
Ziefert, Harriet	*Nicky Upstairs and Downstairs*	1987	Viking
Ziefert, Harriet	*Thank You, Nicky!*	1988	Viking

LEVEL 1: First Grade

Books of this difficulty are read by the average first grader at the end of the school year. The language is more descriptive because it is less repetitive. The vocabulary used in these books is more varied than in earlier levels. Sentence structure is more complex and elaborate as well. Pictures provide less support than in the primer level.

AUTHOR(S)	TITLE	YEAR	PUBLISHER
Alexander, Martha	We're in Big Trouble, Blackboard Bear	1980	Dial Press
Aliki	We Are Best Friends	1982	Greenwillow
Allen, Pamela	Bertie and the Bear	1984	Coward
Barchas, Sarah	I Was Walking down the Road	1975	Scholastic
Barton, Bryon	Airport	1982	Crowell
Barton, Bryon	Building a House	1990	William Morrow
Barton, Bryon	Buzz Buzz Buzz	1973	Macmillan
Barton, Bryon	Hester	1975	Greenwillow
Barton, Bryon	Three Bears	1991	Harper
Bennett, Jill	Teeny Tiny	1986	Putnam
Berenstain, Jan and Stan	Bike Lesson	1964	Beginner Books
Berenstain, Jan and Stan	Old Hat, New Hat	1970	Random House
Brown, Marc	Spooky Riddles	1983	Random House
Brown, Marcia	Three Billy Goats Gruff	1991	HBJ
Brown, Margaret	Goodnight Moon	1947	Harper
Bucknall, Caroline	One Bear All Alone	1986	Dial Press
Burningham, John	Rabbit	1975	Crowell
Butler, Dorothy	My Brown Bear Barney	1989	Greenwillow
Campbell, Rod	Misty's Mischief	1985	Viking
Carle, Eric	Very Busy Spider	1985	Philomel
Causley, Charles	"Quack" Said the Billy Goat	1986	Lippincott
Charlip, Remy	Fortunately	1964	Macmillan
Eastman, Philip D.	Are You My Mother?	1960	Random House
Eastman, Philip D.	Big Dog, Little Dog: A Bedtime Story	1973	Random House
Ehlert, Lois	Planting a Rainbow	1987	HBJ
Flack, Marjorie	Angus and the Cat	1931	Doubleday
Fox, Mem	Hattie and the Fox	1987	Bradbury
Freeman, Don	Rainbow of My Own	1966	Viking
Galdone, Paul	Henny Penny	1979	Houghton Mifflin
Galdone, Paul	Little Tuppen: An Old Tale	1991	Houghton Mifflin
Goenell, Heidi	If I Were a Penguin	1989	Little, Brown
Grindley, Sally	Knock, Knock! Who's There?	1986	Knoff
Guilfoile, Elizabeth	Nobody Listens to Andrew	1957	Modern Curriculum
Hayes, Sarah	This Is the Bear	1986	Harper
Heibroner, Joan	Robert the Rose Horse	1962	Random House
Hill, Eric	Spot's Birthday Party	1962	Random House
Hoff, Syd	Albert and the Albatross	1961	Harper
Hoff, Syd	Oliver	1960	Harper

Level 1 continued

Hurd, Edith T.	*Come and Have Fun*	1962	Harper
Hutchins, Pat	*Good Night Owl*	1990	Simon & Schuster
Hutchins, Pat	*Happy Birthday Sam*	1992	Live Oaks Media
Hutchins, Pat	*My Best Friend*	1993	Greenwillow
Hutchins, Pat	*Tidy Titch*	1991	Greenwillow
Hutchins, Pat	*You'll Soon Grow into Them, Titch*	1983	Greenwillow
Johnson, Crockett	*Picture for Harold's Room*	1960	Harper
Jonas, Ann	*Quilt*	1984	Greenwillow
Jonas, Ann	*Reflections*	1987	Greenwillow
Jonas, Ann	*Trek*	1985	Greenwillow
Jonas, Ann	*Two Bear Cubs*	1982	Greenwillow
Kalan, Robert	*Jump, Frog, Jump!*	1981	Greenwillow
Kline, Suzy	*Don't Touch*	1985	Whitman
Kovalski, Maryann	*Wheels on the Bus*	1990	Little, Brown
Kraus, Robert	*Come Out and Play, Little Mouse*	1995	William Morrow
Kraus, Robert	*Leo the Late Bloomer*	1987	Simon & Schuster
Kraus, Robert	*Where Are You Going, Little Mouse?*	1986	Greenwillow
Kraus, Robert	*Whose Mouse Are You?*	1970	Macmillan
Kuskin, Karla	*Just Like Everyone Else*	1981	Harper
Lopshire, Robert	*Put Me in the Zoo*	1960	Random House
Mayer, Mercer	*Just a Mess*	1987	Western
Mayer, Mercer	*Just Grandma and Me*	1983	Golden Books
Mayer, Mercer	*Just Me and My Dad*	1977	Golden Press
Mayer, Mercer	*Just Me and My Puppy*	1985	Western
Mayer, Mercer	*There's a Nightmare in My Closet*	1968	Dial Press
McLeod, Emilie W.	*Bear's Bicycle*	1975	Little, Brown
McPhail, David	*Bear's Toothache*	1972	Little
McPhail, David	*Fix-It*	1984	Dutton
Minarik, Else H.	*Kiss for Little Bear*	1968	Harper
Nodset, Joan L.	*Who Took the Farmer's Hat?*	1963	Harper
Ormerod, Jan	*Story of Chicken Licken*	1986	Lothrop, Lee & Shepard
Peters, Sharon	*Fun at Camp*	1980	Troll
Peters, Sharon	*Rooster and the Weather Vane*	1988	Troll
Reese, Bob	*Rapid Robert Roadrunner*	1981	Children's Press
Rice, Eve	*Benny Bakes a Cake*	1993	William Morrow
Riddell, Chris	*Ben and the Bear*	1986	Harper
Robart, Rose	*Cake That Mack Ate*	1984	Little, Brown
Rockwell, Anne	*Awful Mess*	1973	Four Winds
Rockwell, Anne	*Tool Box*	1971	Macmillan
Rockwell, Anne	*Trucks*	1984	Dutton
Rosen, Michael	*We're Going on a Bear Hunt*	1989	Simon & Schuster
Sadler, Marilyn	*It's Not Easy Being a Bunny*	1983	Beginner Books
Sendak, Maurice	*Alligators All Around*	1962	Harper
Sendak, Maurice	*Seven Little Monsters*	1977	Harper
Serfozo, Mary	*Who Wants One?*	1989	Simon & Schuster
Seuling, Barbara	*Teeny Tiny Woman*	1978	Puffin Books
Seuss, Dr.	*Great Day for Up*	1974	Random House
Seuss, Dr.	*Green Eggs and Ham*	1960	Random House
Seuss, Dr.	*Hop on Pop*	1963	Random House
Seuss, Dr.	*I Can Read with My Eyes Shut*	1978	Random House
Spier, Peter	*Bored—Nothing to Do!*	1978	Doubleday
Stinson, Kathy	*Red Is Best*	1982	Annick Press
Stone, Rosetta	*Because a Little Bug Went Ka-choo!*	1975	Random House
Taylor, Judy	*My Cat*	1989	Simon & Schuster
Testa, Fulvio	*If You Take a Pencil*	1982	Dial
Tolstoy, Alexei	*Great Big Enormous Turnip*	1968	Watts
Wells, Rosemary	*Noisy Nora*	1973	Dial Books

Wildsmith, Brian	*Animal Tricks*	1980	Oxford
Wood, Audrey	*Napping House*	1984	Harcourt Brace
Ziefert, Harriet	*No Ball Games Here*	1989	Puffin

LEVELS 2-1 and 2-2: Second Grade

Many of the books in these levels have text that is organized into paragraphs. The illustrations in the books enhance the story but provide few specific cues about words in the text. Some of the themes may be closely related to personal experience, but many of these books are about fictional characters and events that are fanciful in nature. Included in this section are poetry books, some simple chapter books, and picture book versions of familiar folk tales.

LEVEL 2-1: Second Grade, first half

AUTHOR(S)	TITLE	YEAR	PUBLISHER
Adoff, Arnold	*Greens*	1988	Lothrop, Lee & Shepard
Ahlberg, Janet and Allan	*Funnybones*	1990	William Morrow
Alexander, Martha	*Blackboard Bear*	1969	Dial Press
Allen, Pamela	*Who Sank the Boat?*	1995	Coward
Asch, Frank	*Bear Shadow*	1985	Prentice-Hall
Asch, Frank	*Bear's Bargain*	1985	Prentice-Hall
Asch, Frank	*Last Puppy*	1980	Prentice-Hall
Berenstain, Stan and Jan	*He Bear, She Bear*	1974	Random House
Bliss, Corinne Demas	*Shortest Kid in the World*	1994	Random House
Bonsall, Crosby N.	*And I Mean It Stanley*	1974	Harper
Bornstein, Ruth L.	*Little Gorilla*	1979	Houghton Mifflin
Bridwell, Norman	*Clifford the Big Red Dog*	1985	Scholastic
Brown, Margaret	*Little Fireman*	1952	Addison-Wesley
Bunting, Eve	*Happy Birthday, Dear Duck*	1988	Clarion
Byars, Betsy	*Beans on the Roof*	1988	Dell
Byars, Betsy	*Go Hush the Baby*	1971	Viking
Carle, Eric	*Very Hungry Caterpillar*	1981	Putnam
Clifton, Lucille	*Some of the Days of Everett Anderson*	1970	Holt
Coerr, Eleanor	*Big Balloon Race*	1981	Harper
Cohen, Miriam	*Don't Eat Too Much Turkey!*	1987	Greenwillow
Cohen, Miriam	*Jim Meets the Thing*	1981	Greenwillow
Cohen, Miriam	*Jim's Dog Muffins*	1984	Greenwillow
Cohen, Miriam	*See You Tomorrow, Charles*	1989	Dell
Croll, Carolyn	*Too Many Babas*	1979	Harper

Level 2-1 continued

Cummings, Pat	*Jimmy Lee Did It*	1985	Lothrop, Lee & Shepard
Dabcovich, Lydia	*Mrs. Huggins and Her Hen Hannah*	1985	Dutton
Degen, Bruce	*Jamberry*	1983	Harper
Delton, Judy	*Birthday Bike for Brimhall*	1995	Dell
DePaola, Tomie	*Charlie Needs a Cloak*	1982	Simon & Schuster
Dubowski, Cathy	*Pretty Good Magic*	1987	Random House
Eastman, Philip D.	*Best Nest*	1968	Beginner Books
Eastman, Philip D.	*Sam the Firefly*	1958	Random House
Ellis, Anne Leo	*Dabble Duck*	1984	Harper
Emberley, Barbara	*Drummer Hoff*	1967	Prentice-Hall
Farley, Walter	*Little Black, A Pony*	1968	Random House
Flack, Marjorie	*Ask Mr. Bear*	1971	Simon & Schuster
Galdone, Paul	*Little Red Hen*	1987	Houghton Mifflin
Galdone, Paul	*Three Bears*	1972	Seabury Press
Gurney, Nancy	*King, the Mice, and the Cheese*	1966	Collins
Harshman, Terry	*Porcupine's Pajama Party*	1985	Harper
Heilbroner, Joan	*Tom the TV Cat*	1984	Random House
Herman, Gail	*Otto the Cat*	1995	Grosset & Dunlap
Hill, Eric	*Spot's First Christmas*	1983	Putnam's
Hoban, Lillian	*Arthur's Christmas Cookies*	1972	Harper
Hoban, Lillian	*Arthur's Honey Bear*	1974	Harper
Hoban, Lillian	*Arthur's Loose Tooth*	1985	Harper
Hoban, Lillian	*Arthur's Pen Pal*	1976	Harper
Hoban, Lillian	*Arthur's Prize Reader*	1978	Harper
Hoban, Lillian	*Case of the Two Masked Robbers*	1986	Harper
Hoff, Syd	*Horse in Harry's Room*	1970	Harper
Hoff, Syd	*Mrs. Brice's Mice*	1988	Harper
Holl, Adelaide	*Rain Puddle*	1965	Lothrop, Lee, & Shepard
Howe, James	*Day the Teacher Went Bananas*	1984	Dutton
Hurd, Edith T.	*Johnny Lion's Book*	1985	Harper
Hutchins, Pat	*Doorbell Rang*	1989	William Morrow
Isadora, Rachel	*Max*	1984	Simon & Schuster
Johnson, Crockett	*Harold and the Purple Crayon*	1981	Harper
Joyce, William	*George Shrinks*	1985	Harper
Kasza, Keiko	*Wolf's Chicken Stew*	1987	Putnam's
Keats, Ezra Jack	*Letter to Amy*	1968	Harper
Keats, Ezra Jack	*Peter's Chair*	1967	Harper
Keats, Ezra Jack	*Snow Day*	1962	Viking
Kessler, E. & L.	*Stan the Hot Dog Man*	1990	Harper
Knight, Joan	*Tickle-Toe Rhymes*	1989	Orchard Books
Krasilovsky, Phyllis	*Man Who Didn't Do His Dishes*	1950	Doubleday
Kraus, Robert	*Milton the Early Riser*	1972	Dutton
Krensky, Stephen	*Three Blind Mice Mystery*	1995	Yearling
Kuskin, Karla	*Soap Soup and Other Verses*	1992	Harper
Lear, Edward	*Owl and the Pussycat*	1991	Dial Books
LeSeig, Theo	*Ten Apples on Top*	1961	Random House
Levinson, Nancy Smiler	*Snowshoe Thompson*	1992	Harper
Lionni, Leo	*Little Blue and Little Yellow*	1959	Astor Honor
Lobel, Anita	*Pancake*	1978	Greenwillow
Lobel, Arnold	*Mouse Soup*	1983	Harper
Lobel, Arnold	*Mouse Tales*	1972	Harper
Lobel, Arnold	*Owl at Home*	1975	Harper
Logan, Dick	*Egg*	1977	Creative
Lord, John Vernon	*Giant Jam Sandwich*	1973	Houghton Mifflin
Marshall, Edward	*Three by the Sea*	1994	Puffin Books
Martin, Bill	*Chicka Chicka Boom Boom*	1989	Simon & Schuster

Mayer, Mercer	*I Was So Mad*	1985	Western
Mayer, Mercer	*Me Too!*	1985	Western
Mayer, Mercer	*There's an Alligator under My Bed*	1987	Dial Press
Mayer, Mercer	*There's Something in My Attic*	1988	Dial Press
Mayer, Mercer	*When I Get Bigger*	1985	Western
McCully, Emily	*Grandma Mix-Up*	1988	Harper
McCully, Emily	*Grandma's at the Lake*	1990	Harper
McGovern, Ann	*Too Much Noise*	1967	Houghton Mifflin
Minarik, Else H.	*Little Bear*	1957	Harper
Minarik, Else H.	*Little Bear's Friend*	1960	Harper
Minarik, Else H.	*Little Bear's Visit*	1961	Harper
Nicoll, Helen	*Meg & Mog*	1976	Viking
Nims, Bonnie L.	*Where Is the Bear?*	1988	Whitman
Parish, Peggy	*Amelia Bedelia*	1992	Harper
Parish, Peggy	*Amelia Bedelia and the Surprise Shower*	1966	Harper
Parish, Peggy	*Amelia Bedelia Goes Camping*	1985	Greenwillow
Parish, Peggy	*Amelia Bedelia Helps Out*	1979	Greenwillow
Parish, Peggy	*Come Back, Amelia Bedelia*	1971	Harper
Parish, Peggy	*Dinosaur Time*	1974	Harper
Parish, Peggy	*Good Work, Amelia Bedelia*	1976	Greenwillow
Parish, Peggy	*Too Many Rabbits*	1974	Macmillan
Paterson, Katherine	*Smallest Cow in the World*	1991	Harper
Peppe, Rodney	*House That Jack Built*	1970	Delacorte
Perkins, Al	*Hand, Hand, Fingers*	1974	Random House
Proger, Annabelle	*Surprise Party*	1977	Pantheon
Rice, Eve	*Sam Who Never Forgets*	1977	Greenwillow
Rose, Gerald	*Trouble in the Ark*	1985	Merrimack
Roy, Ron	*Three Ducks Went Walking*	1979	Scholastic
Rylant, Cynthia	*Henry and Mudge in Puddle Trouble*	1987	Bradbury
Rylant, Cynthia	*Henry and Mudge in the Green Time*	1987	Bradbury
Rylant, Cynthia	*Henry and Mudge, The First Book*	1987	Bradbury
Rylant, Cynthia	*Mr. Putter and Tabby Bake the Cake*	1994	HBJ
Rylant, Cynthia	*Mr. Putter and Tabby Pick the Pears*	1995	HBJ
Rylant, Cynthia	*Mr. Putter and Tabby Pour the Tea*	1994	HBJ
Rylant, Cynthia	*Mr. Putter and Tabby Walk the Dog*	1994	HBJ
Sendak, Maurice	*Where the Wild Things Are*	1963	Harper
Seuss, Dr.	*Cat in the Hat*	1957	Random House
Sharmat, Marjorie Weinman	*Nate the Great*	1977	Dell
Sharmat, Marjorie Weinman	*Nate the Great and the Boring Beach Bag*	1987	Dell
Sharmat, Marjorie Weinman	*Nate the Great and the Fishy Prize*	1985	Dell
Sharmat, Marjorie Weinman	*Nate the Great and the Halloween Hunt*	1990	Dell
Sharmat, Marjorie Weinman	*Nate the Great and the Lost List*	1981	Dell
Sharmat, Marjorie Weinman	*Nate the Great and the Missing Key*	1982	Dell
Sharmat, Marjorie Weinman	*Nate the Great and the Mushy Valentine*	1995	Dell
Sharmat, Marjorie Weinman	*Nate the Great and the Musical Note*	1990	Dell
Sharmat, Marjorie Weinman	*Nate the Great and the Phony Clue*	1977	Coward
Sharmat, Marjorie Weinman	*Nate the Great and the Pillowcase*	1993	Dell

Level 2-1 continued

Sharmat, Marjorie Weinman	*Nate the Great and the Snowy Trail*	1984	Dell
Sharmat, Marjorie Weinman	*Nate the Great and the Sticky Case*	1978	Dell
Sharmat, Marjorie Weinman	*Nate the Great and the Stolen Base*	1994	Dell
Sharmat, Marjorie Weinman	*Nate the Great Goes Down in the Dumps*	1989	Dell
Sharmat, Marjorie Weinman	*Nate the Great Goes Undercover*	1984	Dell
Sharmat, Marjorie Weinman	*Nate the Great Stalks Stupidweed*	1989	Dell
Shulevitz, Uri	*Rain Rain Rivers*	1969	Farrar, Straus & Giroux
Stadler, John	*Adventures of Snail at School*	1993	Harper
Thaler, Mike	*There's a Hippo under My Bed*	1977	Watts
Udry, Janice	*Let's Be Enemies*	1961	Harper
Van Leeuwen, Jean	*More Tales of Amanda Pig*	1985	Dial Press
Vipont, Elfrida	*Elephant and the Bad Baby*	1969	Coward
Walsh, Ellen Stoll	*Mouse Count*	1991	HBJ
Walsh, Ellen Stoll	*Mouse Paint*	1989	HBJ

LEVEL 2-2: Second Grade, second half

AUTHOR(S)	TITLE	YEAR	PUBLISHER
Alder, David A.	*Cam Jansen and the Mystery at the Monkey House*	1993	Puffin
Alder, David A.	*Cam Jansen and the Mystery of Flight 54*	1992	Puffin
Alder, David A.	*Cam Jansen and the Mystery of the Babe Ruth Baseball*	1991	Puffin
Alder, David A.	*Cam Jansen and the Mystery of the Carnival Prize*	1992	Puffin
Alder, David A.	*Cam Jansen and the Mystery of the Circus Clown*	1991	Puffin
Alder, David A.	*Cam Jansen and the Mystery of the Dinosaur Bones*	1991	Puffin
Alder, David A.	*Cam Jansen and the Mystery of the Gold Coins*	1991	Puffin
Alder, David A.	*Cam Jansen and the Mystery of the Monster Movie*	1992	Puffin
Alder, David A.	*Cam Jansen and the Mystery of the Stolen Corn Popper*	1992	Puffin
Alder, David A.	*Cam Jansen and the Mystery of the Stolen Diamonds*	1991	Puffin
Alder, David A.	*Cam Jansen and the Mystery of the Television Dog*	1991	Puffin
Alder, David A.	*Cam Jansen and the Mystery of the U.F.O.*	1991	Puffin
Allard, Harry	*Miss Nelson Is Missing*	1977	Houghton
Allen, Pamela	*Who Sank the Boat?*	1985	Putnam
Arnold, Tedd	*No Jumping on the Bed!*	1987	Dial Press
Asch, Frank	*Happy Birthday Moon*	1982	Prentice-Hall
Bang, Molly	*Wiley and the Hairy Man*	1976	Macmillan
Berenstain, Jan and Stan	*Berenstain Bears' Picnic*	1966	Beginner Books
Berenstain, Stan	*Berenstain Bears' Christmas Tree*	1980	Random House

Bonsall, Crosby N.	*Piggle*	1973	Harper
Brown, Ruth	*Big Sneeze*	1985	Lothrop, Lee & Shepard
Browne, Anthony	*Bear Goes to Town*	1989	Doubleday
Burningham, John	*Mr. Gumpy's Motor Car*	1976	Harper
Burningham, John	*Mr. Gumpy's Outing*	1990	Henry Holt
Cameron, Ann	*More Stories Julian Tells*	1989	Houghton Mifflin
Cameron, Ann	*Stories Julian Tells*	1977	Pantheon
Carle, Eric	*Animals, Animals*	1989	Philomel
Carle, Eric	*Grouchy Ladybug*	1977	Crowell
Christopher, Matt	*Dog That Pitched a No-Hitter*	1988	Little, Brown
Coerr, Eleanor	*Chang's Paper Pony*	1988	Harper
Coerr, Eleanor	*Josefina Story Quilt*	1986	Harper
Cole, Joanna	*Hungry, Hungry Sharks*	1986	Random House
Crowe, Robert L.	*Tyler Toad the Thunder*	1980	Dutton
Delton, Judy	*Pee Wee Scouts: Cookies and Crutches*	1988	Dell
Delton, Judy	*Pee Wees on First*	1995	Dell
Delton, Judy	*Pee Wees on Parade*	1992	Dell
Delton, Judy	*Pee Wees on Skis*	1993	Dell
Delton, Judy	*Pooped Troop*	1989	Dell
DePaola, Tomie	*Art Lesson*	1994	Putnam
Fisher, Aileen	*House of a Mouse*	1988	Harper
Fisher, Aileen	*When It Comes to Bugs*	1983	Harper
Gackenbach, Dick	*Harry & Terrible Whatzit*	1977	Seabury Press
Galdone, Paul	*Gingerbread Boy*	1979	Houghton Mifflin
Galdone, Paul	*Magic Porridge Pot*	1976	Clarion
Galdone, Paul	*Over in the Meadow*	1989	Simon & Schuster
Galdone, Paul	*Three Little Pigs*	1970	Houghton Mifflin
Giff, Patricia Reilly	*All About Stacy*	1988	Dell
Giff, Patricia Reilly	*Candy Corn Contest*	1984	Dell
Giff, Patricia Reilly	*Case of the Cool-Itch Kid*	1989	Dell
Giff, Patricia Reilly	*In the Dinosaur's Paw*	1985	Dell
Giff, Patricia Reilly	*Pickle Puss*	1986	Dell
Giff, Patricia Reilly	*Postcard Pest*	1994	Dell
Giff, Patricia Reilly	*Powder Puff Puzzle*	1992	Dell
Giff, Patricia Reilly	*Say "Cheese"*	1985	Dell
Giff, Patricia Reilly	*Secret at the Polk Street School*	1992	Dell
Giff, Patricia Reilly	*Show Time at the Polk Street School*	1992	Dell
Giff, Patricia Reilly	*Snaggle Doodles*	1985	Dell
Giff, Patricia Reilly	*Spectacular Stone Soup*	1989	Yearling
Giff, Patricia Reilly	*Stacy Says Good-Bye*	1989	Dell
Giff, Patricia Reilly	*Sunny-Side Up*	1986	Dell
Giff, Patricia Reilly	*Wake Up, Emily, It's Mother's Day*	1991	Yearling
Guarino, Deborah	*Is Your Mama a Llama?*	1989	Scholastic
Havill, Juanita	*Jennifer, Too*	1995	Hyperion
Hayes, Geoffrey	*Mystery of the Pirate Ghost*	1985	Random House
Heine, Helme	*Most Wonderful Egg in the World*	1983	Atheneum
Hennessy, B.G.	*Jake Baked the Cake*	1990	Viking
Hoberman, Mary Ann	*A House Is a House for Me*	1978	Viking
Hoberman, Mary Ann	*Yellow Butter Purple Jelly . . .*	1981	Viking
Hogrogian, Nonny	*One Fine Day*	1971	Macmillan
Howe, James	*Pinky and Rex*	1990	Atheneum
Howe, James	*Pinky and Rex and the Spelling Bee*	1991	Atheneum
Hurd, Edith T.	*Stop, Stop*	1961	Harper
Hutchins, Pat	*Don't Forget the Bacon!*	1975	Greenwillow
Hutchins, Pat	*One-Eyed Jake*	1979	Greenwillow
Hutchins, Pat	*Surprise Party*	1986	Simon & Schuster
Hutchins, Pat	*Very Worst Monster*	1985	Greenwillow

Level 2-2 continued

Hutchins, Pat	*Where's the Baby?*	1988	Greenwillow
Hutchins, Pat	*Wind Blew*	1974	Viking
Jeschke, Susan	*Perfect the Pig*	1980	Holt
Jonas, Ann	*Round Trip*	1983	Greenwillow
Keats, Ezra Jack	*Whistle for Willie*	1964	Viking
Kuskin, Karla	*Dogs & Dragons, Trees & Dreams*	1980	Harper
Lear, Edward	*Owl and the Pussy Cat*	1969	Little, Brown
Leverich, Kathleen	*Brigid Beware*	1995	Random House
Leverich, Kathleen	*Brigid Bewitched*	1994	Random House
Leverich, Kathleen	*Brigid the Bad*	1995	Random House
Lewis, Thomas P.	*Hill of Fire*	1971	Harper
Littledale, Freya	*Magic Fish*	1986	Scholastic
Livingston, Myra Cohn	*A Song I Sang to You*	1984	HBJ
Lobel, Arnold	*Frog and Toad Are Friends*	1970	Harper
Lobel, Arnold	*Frog and Toad Together*	1971	Harper
Lobel, Arnold	*Uncle Elephant*	1981	Harper
MacLachlan, P.	*Through Grandpa's Eyes*	1980	Harper
Marshall, James	*George and Martha*	1972	Houghton Mifflin
Marzollo, Jean	*Soccer Sam*	1987	Random House
McCloskey, Robert	*Make Way for Ducklings*	1941	Viking
McGovern, Ann	*Stone Soup*	1968	Scholastic
Merriam, Eve	*A Poem for a Pickle—Funnybone Verses*	1989	Morrow
Merriam, Eve	*Blackberry Ink*	1985	Morrow
Milton, Joyce	*Dinosaur Days*	1985	Random House
Milton, Joyce	*Whales—The Gentle Giants*	1989	Random House
Minarik, Else H.	*Father Bear Comes Home*	1959	Harper
Mueller, Virginia	*Monster Goes to School*	1991	Whitman
Murphy, Jill	*What Next Baby Bear?*	1986	Dial Press
Nicoll, Helen	*Mog at the Zoo*	1982	Heinemann
Nicoll, Helen	*Mog's Mumps*	1976	Heinemann
Oppenheim, Joanne	*You Can't Catch Me!*	1986	Houghton Mifflin
Osborne, Mary Pope	*Afternoon on the Amazon*	1995	Random House
Osborne, Mary Pope	*Dinosaurs Before Dark*	1992	Random House
Park, Barbara	*Junie B. Jones and the Stupid Smelly Bus*	1992	Random House
Park, Barbara	*Junie B. Jones and the Yucky Blucky Fruitcake*	1995	Random House
Preston, Edna Mitchell	*Squawk to the Moon, Little Goose*	1974	Viking
Reinl, Edda	*Three Little Pigs*	1983	Picture Book Studio
Rice, Eve	*Peter's Pockets*	1989	Greenwillow
Rosenbloom, J.	*Deputy Dan Gets His Man*	1985	Random House
Rylant, Cynthia	*Henry and Mudge and the Forever Sea*	1989	Bradbury
Sachar, Louis	*Marvin Redpost: Kidnapped at Birth?*	1992	Random House
Sachar, Louis	*Marvin Redpost: Why Pick on Me?*	1993	Random House
Sandin, Joan	*Pioneer Bear*	1995	Random House
Sendak, Maurice	*Chicken Soup With Rice*	1991	Harper
Sharmat, Marjorie Weinman	*Genghis Khan: Dog-Gone Hollywood*	1995	Random House
Sharmat, Marjorie Weinman	*Gregory, the Terrible Eater*	1985	Macmillan
Slobodkina, Esphyr	*Caps for Sale*	1940	Addison-Wesley
Standiford, Natalie	*Bravest Dog Ever*	1996	Houghton Mifflin
Stanley, Diane	*Conversation Club*	1983	Macmillan
Stevens, Janet	*Three Billy Goats Gruff*	1990	HBJ
Stevenson, James	*"Could Be Worse!"*	1977	Greenwillow
Tresselt, Alvin	*Mitten*	1964	Lothrop, Lee & Shepard
Zemach, Margot	*Little Red Hen*	1987	Farrar, Straus & Giroux
Zolotow, Charlotte	*I Know a Lady*	1984	Greenwillow

APPENDIX B:
A Special Note to Christian Educators

The vast majority of resources designed for parents to help them teach a child to read at home are oriented around phonics techniques. Almost daily, radio listeners hear advertisements for the *Hooked on Phonics* package. My own attendance at home education functions and my reading of home education publications confirms my belief that more than 90% of the available resources have a phonics-first foundation. This is especially true in Christian education. What is it about phonics that makes it so attractive to the home education market? And what is it about other methods that causes concern among Christian educators? A closer look at these questions might help those who are faced with choices about reading instruction to make an informed decision.

Phonics in microcosm: Christian education

My first eight years of teaching were spent in two private Christian schools. The reading curriculum materials that we used were very heavily based in phonics methodology. As anyone in Christian education can tell you, if you are going to purchase a reading series from a Christian publisher, it will probably be centered on phonics. As part of my responsibilities during this time, I developed and administered a home education umbrella program for parents who wanted to teach their children at home. I would meet with these families frequently through the year, consult with them about their program, and oversee the annual testing of their children. These parents used many of the same materials developed for use in Christian day schools, but they also used program materials that were developed specifically for home educators. All of the reading programs used by these families were based heavily on phonics methodology as well.

When I first got a teaching assignment in a public school as a remedial reading teacher, I began to hear about other models of reading instruction that were not oriented around phonics techniques. I was very skeptical of these approaches. After all, Rudolph Flesch in his books *Why Johnny Can't Read* (1955) and *Why Johnny Still Can't Read* (1981) had convinced me that look-say reading methods had failed miserably in our nation's public schools. But what my colleagues and college professors were recommending was totally different from sight reading, look-say programs. What they recommended was teaching reading from the top down—teaching children to read in much the same way that they had so efficiently learned to talk.

I was intrigued. I asked about research. I asked about look-say. I asked about phonics. I got answers that I was excited about. I studied and learned more. And as I began to integrate elements of a language-centered approach into my own instruction, I saw children get excited about books while they were becoming proficient readers.

About this time, I had the opportunity to receive the yearlong training that it took to become a Reading Recovery teacher. Reading Recovery is an intensive early-intervention program designed to help at-risk first graders become proficient in reading before they fall hopelessly behind. (This highly-effective program is discussed in detail in Chapter 4.) The results I saw were truly amazing. Reading Recovery uses relatively little isolated phonics instruction; rather, general phonics principles are taught in the context of real reading and writing.

I was nearing the end of my Master's program at Ohio State University, and I decided to write my thesis about reading instruction in Christian schools. I wanted to find out why teachers in most Christian day and home schools use phonics as their primary method of reading instruction. Given all the research that suggests that other approaches can work at least as well, what are the theoretical and philosophical reasons that Christian educators give for sticking so strictly to phonics methods? The answers to this question could provide clues as to why phonics instruction techniques are viewed and used with such reverence not only in Christian education, but in other more "conservative" circles as well (Thogmartin, 1994).

As I compiled information written by theologians and theorists, and as I interviewed my fellow Christian educators in all levels of education, I discovered that most opinions were formed from "guilt by association." These educators associated nonphonics methods with non-Christian men like John Dewey, a progressive educator and a signer of the *First Humanist Manifesto*. They associated the more natural learning styles used by top-down educators with a lack of discipline. They associated whole language with look-say methods that had gotten much bad press from Christian writers. They associated the philosophy espoused and jargon used by top-down writers with a lack of reverence for the written word, and with a lack of scholarship in general.

Positive associations were also made between phonics methods and traditional values. Godly men like William McGuffey and Daniel Webster, who were very influential in promoting a Judaeo-Christian ethic in early American public education, used simple phonics principles in their textbooks. The "back to basics" call of the early 1980's is still a rallying cry for Christian educators, and phonics is considered by them to be one foundational building block of the movement. Phonics instruction is associated with the more disciplined environment found in most Christian school classrooms. And probably most important of all, the high reading scores achieved by the average Christian school student are directly associated with the phonics curriculum used from his or her earliest minutes in school.

Although these associations were made by writers and by people I interviewed, not once did anyone suggest that nonphonics methods were inherently evil. There is nothing in the methodology used in whole language classrooms, for example, that is considered wrong. But the movement as a whole is perceived by many Christians as being based on humanistic philosophies. Many have a gut feeling that the New Age movement (a popular semireligious belief system that incorporates many teachings from Eastern religions) is somehow connected with the whole language philosophy. I believe that these impressions are just that—impressions.

I personally maintain a Christian world view. Once I separated impressions from the way things really are, I could see many good things that a book-centered philosophy of reading instruction had to offer. And I know many professing Christian educators who agree. To reject or accept a method, idea, or invention simply because of impressions like those above is neither wise nor prudent. The computer I am using to type these words is made of components developed by an astounding cross-section of people from all faiths and persuasions. And yet, who could deny its usefulness and benefits? Perhaps in the area of reading instruction, as in computing, we should be willing to look for the positive and beneficial things while using discretion about our concerns.

As I mentioned before, many people whom I interviewed based their positive feelings about phonics curricula on the positive results they were seeing. It is generally true that most Christian schools use phonics, and it is also generally true that most Christian schools boast high scores on standardized reading tests.

But should phonics instruction be given all the credit? It is quite possible that other factors are at work that contribute to these high test scores. Generally speaking, Christian families are oriented around written material because of their high regard for the Scriptures. Most Christian leaders encourage the daily reading of the Bible, both personally and in family group settings. Therefore, most children from Christian homes have grown up in a setting where reading is a highly valued part of everyday life. They come to school already having experienced the kind of environment that reading teachers consider to be optimal. When the teacher begins to present letters and sounds in a phonics curriculum, these children can usually relate them easily to what they already know about reading.

Contrast the above situation with children who come to school having few positive experiences with print. They have not seen their parents reading books, magazines, or the newspaper, nor have they had the joy of hearing stories read aloud. They may never have watched programs like *Sesame Street,* nor listened to story books on tape. If they go to school and immediately are confronted with letters and sounds, they lack the appropriate preparatory experiences. These children, unlike the children from the average Christian family, need to be given an expanded experience base with books and literature right from the start of their school careers. Because this scenario is more common in public schools than in Christian schools, it is not appropriate to claim that the method of reading instruction used in Christian schools is the sole reason for higher reading scores.

Another factor that comes into play has to do with the general clientele not only of Christian schools, but of most private schools as well. It is usually true that those who are paying tuition (on top of the taxes that we all pay to support our schools) are more involved with their children's education because they have more invested. Or, conversely, they invest more because they are more involved. In any case, most teachers will agree that parental support is a major positive factor in a child's school achievement. Again, most children who attend Christian schools have this advantage, so they usually realize higher achievement in all subject areas, and not only in reading.

In Chapter 1, I make the point that a phonics curriculum based on drill and workbook exercises more closely matches the style of questioning used on the average achievement test. Higher scores are always achieved when the testing style matches the instructional style. Consider for a moment the advantage that students who write every day, as part of their reading instruction, might have when taking an essay test.

If it's working, why change it?

Good question. I once heard a top-down theorist say that students who have lots of support in the classroom and at home will learn in spite of the method used. I believe that he is right. But often, a student's personal learning style does not fit well with the mode of instruction. Consider Nicole in the fictional scenario from Chapter 1. She began to flounder when a segmented, drill-oriented reading program was used. In my own research, I talked with a mother who was totally frustrated with her fourth-grade son. She had home-schooled him from the beginning. She shared with me that he was at least two grade levels behind in reading and, not surprisingly, he hated to read. I asked her what kind of reading instruction program she had used. She had started with one phonics package, and when he was not progressing as he should, she switched to another. They were now on their third phonics program and he was still struggling. I felt sorry for that boy! Would he ever learn that reading was any more than parroting sounds and memorizing rules? Would he ever look forward to sitting down with a good book and just enjoying it? This is the result of not matching the instructional mode to the student.

I maintain that not all students will learn best with a packaged phonics program. The best learning-to-read program will be one that changes with the needs of the child instead of expecting the child to adjust to it. The reading materials used (preferably real books) will vary with the child's interests and needs. A production line model of education seen in most schools is extremely inefficient when dealing with students who find it difficult to adapt to its demands. Because the success of the typical phonics approach demands strict adherence to a sequenced series of memorized sounds and rules, there is little, if any, room for variation based on the needs of the learner. If a child finds this bottom-up approach to be boring and meaningless, Mom or Dad may need to turn his "bottom up" to encourage him to stick with it!

A challenge . . .

I'd like to challenge my teaching colleagues in Christian day and home schools to consider the information presented in this book. The approach I recommend does not minimize the importance of learning letters and their associated sounds. The successes achieved by those who are using these methods have been verified by much research and experience. As you read, you may discover a way to teach reading that is more in line with your lifestyle and what you really believe!

If you'd like to read more about reading instruction from this perspective, I'd like to recommend *Language Arts in Christian Schools* by Robert Bruinsma (1990). In this book, Bruinsma talks about teaching reading using what he calls a *language-centered* approach. I'd also like to recommend an article he wrote, in response to my research discussed above, titled "Phonics and the Teaching of Reading in Christian Schools" (Bruinsma, 1994). In this article, Bruinsma provides more insight into the philosophies that drive the techniques we use in reading instruction.

REFERENCES

Adams, M.J. (1990). *Beginning to read: Thinking and learning about print.* Urbana, IL: University of Illinois, Center for the Study of Reading.

Anderson, R.C., Hiebert, E.H., Scott, J., & Wilkinson, I. (1985). *Becoming a nation of readers.* Washington, DC: The National Institute of Education.

Anderson, W.W., Fordham, A.E. (1991). Issues in education: Beware of "magic" phonics programs. *Childhood Education, 68(1),* 8–9.

Blumenfeld, S.L. (1973). *How to tutor.* New York: Arlington House.

Bruinsma, R. (1990). *Language Arts in Christian Schools.* Grand Rapids: Christian Schools International.

Bruinsma, R. (1994). Phonics and the teaching of reading in Christian schools. *Journal of Research on Christian Education, 3(2),* 285–295.

Burke, C. (1972). The language process: Systems or systematic? In Hodges and Rudorf (Eds.) *Language and learning to read: What teachers should know about language,* 24–31. Boston: Houghton Mifflin.

Carbo, M. (1988). Debunking the great phonics myth. *Phi Delta Kappan, 70(3),* 226–240.

Chall, J.S. (1989). Learning to read: The great debate 20 years later—A response to "Debunking the great phonics myth." *Phi Delta Kappan, 70(7),* 521–538.

Clay, M.M. (1966). Emergent reading behavior. Doctoral dissertation, University of Auckland, New Zealand.

Clay, M.M. (1985). *The early detection of reading difficulties* (3rd ed.). Auckland, New Zealand: Heinemann.

Clay, M.M. (1993a). *An observation survey of early literacy achievement.* Auckland, New Zealand: Heinemann.

Clay, M.M. (1993b). *Reading Recovery: A guidebook for teachers in training.* Auckland, New Zealand: Heinemann.

Crain-Thoreson, C., Dale, P.S. (1992). Do early talkers become early readers? Linguistic precocity, preschool language, and emergent literacy. *Developmental Psychology, 28(3),* 421–429.

Dobson, J. (1995). Dr. Dobson answers your questions. *Focus on the Family, 19(7),* 5.

Elkonian, D.B. (1973). "U.S.S.R." in J. Downing (Ed.), *Comparative reading.* New York: Macmillan. 551–580.

Flesch, R. (1955). *Why Johnny can't read and what you can do about it.* New York: Harper & Row.

Flesch, R. (1981). *Why Johnny still can't read: A new look at the scandal of our schools.* New York: Harper & Row.

Goodman, K. (1986). *What's whole in whole language?* Portsmouth, NH: Heinemann.

Gunning, T. (1995). Word building: A strategic approach to the teaching of phonics. *The Reading Teacher. 48(6),* 484–488.

Hunt, G. (1989). *Honey for a child's heart* (3rd ed.). Grand Rapids: Zondervan.

Kobrin, B. (1995). *Eyeopeners II.* New York: Scholastic.

Pinnell, G.S., DeFord, D.E., & Lyons, C.A. (1988). *Reading Recovery: Early intervention for at-risk first graders.* Arlington, VA: Educational Research Service.

Rhodes, L. (1981). I can read! Predictable books as resources for reading and writing instruction. *Reading Teacher, 34(5),* 511–518.

Smith, F. (1986). *Insult to intelligence: The bureaucratic invasion of our classrooms.* New York: Arbor House.

Smith, F. (1988). *Understanding reading: A psycholinguistic analysis of reading and learning to read.* Fourth edition. Hillsdale, NJ: Lawrence Erlbaum Associates.

Stanovich, Keith E. (1994). Romance and reality. *Reading Teacher, 47(4),* 280–291.

Strickland, D.S. (1990). Emergent literacy: How young children learn to read and write. *Educational Leadership, 47(6),* 18–23.

Swartz, S., & Klein, A. (Eds.). (1997). *Research in Reading Recovery.* Portsmouth, NH: Heinemann.

Thogmartin, M. (1994). The prevalence of phonics instruction in fundamentalist Christian schools. *Journal of Research on Christian Education, 3(1),* 103–130.

Thomas, K.F. (1985). Early reading as a social interaction process. *Language Arts, 62(5),* 469–475.

Trelease, J. (1995). *The read-aloud handbook* (4th ed.). New York: Penguin.

Tunnell, M.O., Jacobs, J.H. (1989). Using "real" books: Research findings on literature based reading instruction. *Reading Teacher, 42(7),* 470–477.

Turner, R.L. (1989). The "great" debate: Can both Carbo and Chall be right? *Phi Delta Kappan, 71(4),* 276–283.

INDEX

About
the Author

Mark B. Thogmartin is
the former headmaster of a
private Christian school
where he also adminis-
tered a home education
program. He has taught
students for over sixteen
years in both public and
private schools and holds
a master's degree in read-
ing. He is currently pursuing a doctoral degree at Andrews
University and teaches reading and mathematics at Walnut
Township Schools in his hometown of Millersport, Ohio,
where he resides with his wife, Donna, and their three boys.